*From Brass Hat
to Bowler Hat*

From Brass Hat
to Bowler Hat

Major-General
Sir Francis de Guingand
K.B.E., C.B., D.S.O.

HAMISH HAMILTON
LONDON

First published in Great Britain 1979
by Hamish Hamilton Ltd
Garden House 57–59 Long Acre London WC2E 9JL

Published in the United States of America by Hamish Hamilton in
association with David & Charles Inc, North Pomfret, Vermont 05053, USA

British Library Cataloguing in Publication Data
De Guingand, *Sir* Francis
   From brass hat to bowler hat
   1. De Guingand, *Sir* Francis 2. Great Britain.
   Army—Biography 2. Generals—Great Britain
   —Biography
   I. Title
   355.3'32'0924   DA69.3.G/   78–41227

   ISBN 0–241–10165–4

Printed in Great Britain by
Bristol Typesetting Co Ltd, Barton Manor, St Philips, Bristol

Contents

List of Illustrations

Foreword

I have so often been asked to describe my experiences after I left the British Army in 1947 that I hope I shall be forgiven for writing this small book of memoirs to complement my previous wartime accounts, *Operation Victory* and *Generals at War*.

Many of the great wartime leaders went on to positions of prestige and dignity within the British Empire. But what happens to the humble Chief of Staff after the great armies dwindle and demobilize? My opposite number, that charming and efficient soldier Walter Bedell Smith who was Eisenhower's Chief of Staff, became American Ambassador to Moscow, but his health was permanently marred by the responsibilities he carried in the war, and he sadly did not live long.

My own health gave cause for complaint; but having chosen to leave the Army and try my luck in industry I was privileged to lead a long and varied career in civilian life—and to retain my friendship with my two wartime bosses, Eisenhower and Montgomery. Here, then, is my story.

F. de Guingand. Cannes, 1978.

Chapter One

Chief of Staff

I was born in February 1900 near London, where my father owned a manufacturing business. In time I was sent away to school at Ampleforth in Yorkshire. From there I went as a Prize Cadet to Sandhurst, where I passed out at the age of nineteen and was commissioned Second Lieutenant in the second battalion of the Prince of Wales's Own West Yorkshire Regiment. After a year on the north-west frontier of India I was posted to our first battalion at Cork in Southern Ireland—where the Brigade-Major happened to be Captain (Brevet-Major) B. L. Montgomery DSO, a distinguished company commander and staff officer of the Great War.

Later, when our battalion returned to Yorkshire at the end of the Irish troubles in 1923, Captain Montgomery appeared once more in our midst—this time as a staff officer (GSO2) of our 49th Territorial Division, living at our regimental depot mess when in York.

As Montgomery's brother Brian has testified, the influence of this passionate soldier was felt wherever he went, especially among subalterns and junior officers. I came to know him very well since we were both engaged in the training of young Territorials. It was no surprise to us when he was appointed Instructor at the Staff College, Camberley, in 1926, having at last been promoted to full majority. However, we were surprised to hear of his marriage the following year as he had always preached celibacy as the pre-requisite of military ambition! 'You can't make a good soldier and a good husband,' had been his constant maxim.

Betty Carver proved a dear and devoted wife to Montgomery—and there is no doubt in my mind that if she had lived, many of Montgomery's less endearing characteristics might have been subdued. Certainly he was shaken to his very core when she died in 1937.

By then I knew him intimately, having served on exercises as his Brigade-Major in the Suez Canal zone. Strange to say—since Montgomery's reputation is so firmly rooted in his iron discipline and cautiousness as a commander—I found from the beginning that side by side with meticulous professionalism went a certain tendency to make hasty decisions, as much on the field as off it. Perhaps it was this very impulsiveness—which more than once threatened his career in the inter-war period—which it was my privilege to perceive and often to mitigate as his Chief of Staff.

However, such things belonged to the future—though doubtless they were fatefully rehearsed in the Canal Brigade exercise of 1933 when, under the eyes of Tim Pile, our Brigadier, Montgomery and I attempted to locate and bring to battle an 'enemy force'. As we could not locate these forces I was loath to alter our disposition; but by nightfall Montgomery became impatient and prepared orders for our own force to set out. It was only by perseverance and good fortune that I managed at last to get an RAF aeroplane to reconnoitre on our behalf; and to my intense relief it sighted our 'enemy' in laager for the night not far away. I had managed to persuade Montgomery to await the plane's return; and with this information we were subsequently able to rout our opponents, thus earning Montgomery considerable kudos. It may well have implanted in Montgomery's mind the seeds of our later association in 'real' war.

Such a prospect became increasingly likely as the 1930s progressed. Montgomery became a teacher once more—this time as Chief Instructor at the Staff College, Quetta, where my regiment was stationed, and whence Montgomery helped to engineer my entry to the Staff College, Camberley. He may well have been utilitarian in his many kindnesses at that time and later; but no one can deny that his furthering the fortunes of so many junior officers was to bear remarkable fruit.

In my own case, I would have preferred to become OC troops in Nyasaland and Tanganyika, a post which I had been offered by the Colonial Office. But my Brigadier and Montgomery both urged—if not ordered me—to go to Camberley. Thereafter my career was oddly preparatory for the eventual position I was to hold. In 1937 I became Brigade-Major to the Commandant of the Small Arms School at Netheravon, and after much badgering the War Office allowed me—at my own expense—to visit both my French and German counterparts at Mourmelon and Dobrietz. I must have earned a slight reputation, for in June 1939 I was selected to become Military Assistant to the Secretary of State for War, Hore-Belisha. Undoubtedly this was an education in how to serve a difficult and ambitious master; for though I came to admire Hore-Belisha both as a man and a courageous minister I was soon exercising the utmost diplomacy in ironing out the strains induced by his sometimes rough-shod riding in the War Office and the Army. I was also forced to learn that difficult art—since, like Montgomery, Hore-Belisha disliked reading official papers and preferred a personal résumé—of sifting information and delivering verbal synopses. When war was declared I moved into an office with Hore-Belisha's Principal Private Secretary, and was thus able to witness the interplay of military, political and personal factors in the 'room at the top'. At the end of 1939 Generals Gort and Ironside, and the Permanent Under-Secretary, P. J. Grigg, turned against their political master; and in the subsequent in-fighting Hore-Belisha was forced out of office. Because of my inside knowledge I too was banished, under protest, to the Staff College at Haifa, instead of taking command of a battalion of my regiment at York. However even in Haifa I was silenced, for the Commandant felt that my weekly 'progress reports' on the war were considered demoralizing rather than illuminating—and for a time I was actually placed under arrest. I predicted, for example, that France would fall to the Germans in three weeks. There were a number of red faces that summer in Haifa when my prediction proved correct!

The collapse of the Allies in Scandinavia and France did however push war in my direction. In December 1940 General Richard O'Connor launched his brilliant desert offensive and trounced the Italians in Cyrenaica. That month, having just been made Commandant of the School of Combined Operations, I was posted to the Joint Planning Staff in Cairo; and from there and from various vantage points in Greece and the Aegean I was to have a ringside view of the battle for the Mediterranean. I witnessed Wavell's star rise as a result of O'Connor's desert victories; and fall as he allowed British forces to be removed from O'Connor's command and directed them to 'Eden's folly' in Greece and the subsequent débâcle in Crete. Here was a model of how not to squander limited resources and men. Wavell's judgement was all

3

at sea. He permitted political considerations to override sound military judgement when the outcome was predictably hopeless; and protested against political pressure when, in the case of Iraq and Syria, the outcome was, militarily speaking, certain of success. None of us in Cairo were surprised to see him go; indeed it is a matter of considerable amusement to see how little historians have pointed the accusing finger at such second-rate performances, while begrudging the real achievements of less amiable and less obvious gentlemen.

Auchinleck was a very different case. Montgomery detested him, and was wont to declare that 'his face was his fortune'. But then Montgomery was wont to admire those—like Wavell and, at first, Alexander—who gave him his head; whereas Auchinleck, when he was Monty's Commanding Officer in 1940, was unwise enough to cross him : a fact which, as will be seen, Monty never forgave.

This was a shame, for Auchinleck's contribution to ultimate British victory in the Western Desert is undeniable to anyone who, as I did, served in that theatre during those fateful years. Auchinleck restored morale in the Desert Force, and under his distinctive leadership his newly named Eighth Army launched an offensive in November 1941 that relieved Tobruk, captured Benghazi and threatened Agheila. When Rommel subsequently counter-attacked, and in the spring of 1942 pushed the Eighth Army back to Alamein, it was Auchinleck's personal assumption of command that restored the situation and paved the way for the successful defence of Alam Halfa. He had, over a period of some eleven months, overseen the security of the Middle East from Syria to India, and kept the Eighth Army intact and Rommel at bay. His selection of subordinates was his ultimate undoing, for, though he had an eye for potential, his sense of timing and that careful nurturing of talent that characterized Montgomery's genius was wholly absent. He made me Director of Military Intelligence in February 1942 when I had no experience whatever of such duties. Again, in July 1942 he made me Brigadier in charge of his General Staff at Eighth Army HQ, when the only experience I had of such a top staff appointment in the field was that of visitor. Such gestures of faith showed courage but surely not wisdom at such a critical moment in our country's fortunes.

Nevertheless the experience I gained was to prove invaluable

4

to me, and perhaps even to Eighth Army—though Auchinleck would not be there to harvest the rewards. For on 13 August 1942 Lieutenant-General Bernard Montgomery met me at the cross-roads outside Alexandria and—two days before he was entitled to—assumed command of the Eighth Army in Egypt.

Montgomery's takeover in the Western Desert in the summer of 1942 must surely rank as one of the great military perform-ances of all time. The subsequent cavilling by historians at what they consider to be Montgomery's over-inflated reputation is surely disingenuous, or at worst envious; for here, to those who were fortunate enough to find themselves in Egypt at that moment, was a quite obvious turning-point: a moment when history—that curious compound of interacting forces—devolves seemingly on to one man. There can be no doubt, despite the achievements of Auchinleck from October 1941 to August 1942, that the Eighth Army was tired, in great need of retraining, and was digging in with one eye over its shoulder. Whether at platoon level or the offices of the various army HQs, there was an air of uncertainty. Rommel had been halted—but only until he built up sufficient reserves to plunge on again. The initiative rested with the Afrika Corps; and though the defensive strengths of Alam Halfa were recognized, there was no certainty that Rommel would be stopped. Even Hitler later referred to this as the 'Golden Age', when the collapse of Egypt seemed probable, the fulfil-ment of his Mediterranean dream.

Alexander, charming and unperturbed, would no doubt have conducted the same cool evacuation from the Nile delta as he had at Dunkirk if Rommel had proved victorious; but this time his erstwhile Dunkirk colleague was in a very different frame of mind. Instead of a corps, Montgomery now commanded an army; instead of being severed from his allies and outflanked, he held the sole access to Alexandria and Cairo. It was a terrain which, from his years as a battalion commander in the early 1930s, he knew well. It was inconceivable to him that Rommel, with his extended lines of communication, could really threaten Cairo. Yet the evidence was unmistakable: files burning, con-tingency plans for a withdrawal, evacuation of women and children . . .

The situation was one in which fresh blood was undoubtedly required. 'Strafer' Gott, Churchill's first choice, would have been

5

disastrous and no doubt have given Churchill the opportunity for more Dunkirk rhetoric. Auchinleck himself wanted Montgomery, strange to say; but their partnership would have been a difficult one. Alexander was the perfect foil to Montgomery in those days : a C-in-C who needed to give no strategic directive and who was prepared to back his general in the field to the hilt.

However, it was not simply fresh blood that made Montgomery's name. Montgomery was cruel and unjust in denying the soldiers of Eighth Army their Africa Star for service before August 1942, but there can be no doubt that he forged a new weapon, and he acknowledged no debt to others. Here was no trained, brave army awaiting fresh inspiration. Under Auchinleck the Eighth Army might just have stopped Rommel at Alam Halfa; but it is frankly impossible to envisage its metamorphosis into the tough, unyielding army that smashed its way back to Tunis. This transformation was Montgomery's achievement, and historiography will be in poor hands if ever this is forgotten.

There was nothing accidental or even lucky in Montgomery's takeover on 13 August 1942. Undistinguished at school, scandalously behaved at Sandhurst, Montgomery had then set himself to the wheel and his sheer professionalism was proverbial in the army. He was not renowned for his advanced ideas, and humanly speaking was considered something of a misfit. What would make him a figure of such historical dimension was a quality which no other British field commander has demonstrated in the same way since Wellington : a vision, brilliantly communicated, of what an army should be. It is in this sense that he felt he was right to refuse Auchinleck's army its Africa Star; in this sense that his victories must be viewed historically. He would make mistakes, miss opportunities, misjudge people, perhaps fail in magnanimity when reaching the pinnacle of success. But the things he did were not pragmatic, nor were his failings accidental. He had made himself, despite being an infantryman, master in every military department; had studied his profession and worked industriously as a leader and trainer of men for almost thirty years before fate finally presented him with the opportunity to execute his vision. He played to more and bigger galleries as time went on; but that essential vision remained constant and grew only in profundity. He assumed command of the assault on Normandy—by far the greatest seaborne invasion that will surely ever take place in human history—in the same way that he had grasped the reins of Auchinleck's army in the desert in 1942. He might upset some by the ruthlessness of his decisions—as in the sacking of those whom he considered inefficient or disliked—but the imprint of his command was unmistakable and has dominated the British Army ever since. Professionalism was, at last, in; brave amateurishness was out.

How well I remember those strange first days when Montgomery took over in the desert! Knowing him as I did, I doubted whether he would tolerate such an inexperienced staff officer in charge of his General Staff; and indeed he did warn me not to be disappointed if he brought out a tried and trusted man from England. I presumed this to be 'Simbo' Simpson, who had been his Brigade-Major at Portsmouth before the war.

Simpson, though blessed with a distinctively clear brain like Montgomery himself, was perhaps too much like his master to be the foil Montgomery needed in the field; and he remained at the War Office for the rest of the war, and thereafter as a loyal Vice-Chief of the Imperial General Staff.

But what could I offer this highly professional and somewhat ruthless new army commander? I was a temporary Brigadier; a banished Military Assistant from the office of the Secretary of State for War; a silenced Staff College teacher; a disregarded Joint Planner; an ex-regimental soldier thrust without experience into the post of DMI, Middle East, and then placed in charge of the General Staff of an army in which I had never actually served.

Perhaps war is the ultimate catalyst. Though I felt humbled by Montgomery's intention to get out a replacement for me from England, I was not disheartened. Life revolves around personalities more than factors, and I enjoyed being in the Mediterranean. I had many friends at HQ; in Cairo and as DMI I had enjoyed the confidence of many officers in Eighth Army. I suppose, in truth, I loved my work, even under war conditions. I had a gambling instinct—which had, and would, cost me dear!—and a certain native optimism. I gave Montgomery a verbal précis of the situation as we drove out to Eighth Army at 7 a.m. that morning in August and then watched with astonishment and admiration the way Montgomery set about his new task. If I had wondered, in the car, what the General was thinking of me, I now

7

put such preoccupations aside. Here was a commander who knew his own mind, a man of destiny: a man I could serve.

Today, in our age of high technology and bottomless egotism, the concept of creating a team may seem impossibly outdated. Yet if Montgomery was ruthlessly professional, he was also a student of character. He rarely forgot a name or overlooked a talent; and he had a positive genius for 'bringing on' young officers, moving them from post to post and responsibility to responsibility in the way a first-class farmer tends his fields and rotates his crops. This 'thinking ahead' was such a distinctive hallmark of Montgomery's leadership that it is surprising historians have paid so little attention to it. Even the most brilliant operations staff officers were turned out to serve time at the front in an active capacity. Not only did this make for better and more battle-experienced staff officers, but it also avoided the notion that to serve on the commander's staff was better than service in the field. In retrospect it was an extraordinary achievement of Montgomery's to create an army in which there was great mobility of rank and responsibility—and which yet effused such brilliant specialists: intelligence experts, engineers, inventors, scientific advisers, administrators. I do not think such an achievement could have been possible unless, under inspired leadership, a team spirit had evolved in which individual considerations were subordinated confidently to the common cause. Montgomery rightly saw that in order to produce this spirit he must produce victories; and it is salutary to think that he fought the battle of Alam Halfa after only a bare fortnight in command.

What a morale-booster the battle turned out to be! How simple—and how serenely predicted by the army commander himself. After that we never looked back; indeed Montgomery was so grateful to me that he awarded me the DSO immediately afterwards—a decoration I hardly felt I deserved.

Surely no other field commander could, within six weeks, have then reversed the role of his army so completely from defence to offence. Our attempt, at the climax of Alam Halfa, to pounce on Rommel had proved costly and ineffective; yet by the last week in October we possessed an army capable of fighting—and winning—one of the great set-piece battles of military history. Could any other commander have done it? Historians may carp at Montgomery's subsequent failure to deliver the *coup de grâce*;

8

but the authority with which Montgomery planned, trained and commanded the Eighth Army at the Battle of Alamein had to be seen to be believed. By comparison Alam Halfa was child's play, for it involved only minor casualties. Certain critics have claimed that the outcome of the Battle of Alamein was inevitable, that it was a battle of attrition in which quantity was bound to win the day; and that Rommel was hampered by the lesser fighting abilities of his Italian allies, and his shortage of supplies.

To assert all this is, however, to miss the point. To break Rommel's seemingly impregnable position at Alamein, screened by vast minefields and without flanks, required an offensive capacity—in leadership, arms and men—which Britain had simply not yet managed to produce in Hitler's war. There had been limited successes; imaginative generalship at times, and courage shown in defeat. But to plan and execute a battle in which you *expect* to lose over 10,000 men in casualties at a critical moment in your country's fortunes, requires generalship of the very highest order—and this Montgomery displayed. No wonder Churchill's Cabinet grew anxious, and the atmosphere at the War Office in London grew tense. Churchill had urged an offensive at the earliest possible moment, had even sacked Auchinleck to get it. But when the crunch came, was it wise to risk our only coherent force left in the Middle East? How easy it would be for Rommel to sweep on to Cairo and Alexandria if we failed! Would the Americans be willing to go ahead with their landings in North Africa if Axis forces held the entire north coast of the continent?

Moreover, what was this British force known as Eighth Army? Was it not merely a polyglot mass of different nationalities, from Poles to South Africans, from Indians to Australians, from Gurkhas to New Zealanders? How could they be welded together into a human force willing to fight and die for a few miles of sandy desert?

Rommel himself, we now know, was aware of the vital importance of this battle—as was Hitler.

Were we, at Eighth Army HQ? I think it is a measure of Montgomery's genius as a commander that we were not. Or rather, though we acknowledged its importance and sent out the army commander's personal message to the troops on the eve of the battle, we didn't seriously imagine we could fail. And when

9

things didn't go quite as smoothly as we, in our heady confidence, had envisaged there in his caravan at the seat of the power was a commander whose iron self-discipline, whose absolute conviction that we would succeed, roused even the most faint-hearted.

El Alamein was the proving ground of British military renascence in the Second World War. Without it one frankly cannot imagine the feats which were subsequently achieved. Behind us stretched a pathetic catalogue of bungled efforts and ultimate failures: the defence of Belgium, Dunkirk, Norway, Greece, Crete, Dieppe, and the loss of North Africa to the very gates of Cairo. Democracy had shown itself a poor opponent on the field of battle, when one must be willing to lay down one's life. However demonic, Hitler had certainly inculcated an almost suicidal determination among his adopted people; and even the Italian soldiers were encouraged to display great courage by the example of Rommel's German troops.

To break into Rommel's stronghold, to tempt forth his armour, destroy it and so win the day, required an equal determination. Few historians have acknowledged the ruthless grip with which Montgomery conducted the battle: the threats to sack certain officers in the field—the most humiliating of all ends to a military career—unless they showed more determined leadership. Montgomery has been accused of First World War tactics; but how little do such criticisms reflect the reality of those October days and nights. On the contrary, the great offensives of the Western Front had petered out in futile gains of ground, if at all; whereas it was Montgomery's absolute and unrelenting desire to smash Rommel's army which characterized his generalship at that moment. Certain subordinate generals would have liked to conserve their forces and preserve their precious armour; moreover, there was a limit to which one could commit the troops of small Empire nations without risking the ruin of their only trained means of national defence. As the days and nights passed it became very much a duel of wills—perhaps more so than in any other battle fought during the war. The months of bitter fighting in Normandy two years later called for resolution and great leadership; but no Allied general ever lost faith in our ultimate victory. El Alamein was very different; and if I had not really 'earned' my DSO from Alam Halfa, I think I earned it in the raging sequel. When, on the second night, it seemed important—

if not essential—for the army commander to force our hesitant and already battle-weary army back into action across the Miteiriya Ridge, I summoned General Leese and General Lumsden and woke Montgomery. It was about 3.30 a.m. when Montgomery spoke to them, as well as to the commander of the 10th Armoured Division by telephone; and this conference set the tone for the rest of the battle. What might have been the prelude to stalemate was instead an exemplary demonstration of Montgomery's greatness as a general. Our offensive was renewed; and when, later, the Minister of State, Richard Casey, came to my HQ to show a telegram he had prepared, warning Churchill to expect a reverse, I was very angry indeed; and promised it would be the end of his political career if he sent it.

In the circumstances, it is considerably to Montgomery's credit that at the high point of the battle he allowed me to alter the final thrust he had in mind. The battle had become a test of nerve and of will; it would have been quite understandable if he had ordered the thrust to proceed according to plan in the same way that he had ordered our reluctant commanders back into the initial fray. Here again I felt I was beginning to earn my keep as his Chief of Staff; and that our relationship was becoming a two-way process. The manner in which he entrusted complete authority to me as his Chief of Staff was almost frightening, considering that I had never actually commanded a battalion other than the King's African Rifles; but such trust emboldened me to pluck up courage and speak my true mind. I had discussed the alteration of the 'Supercharge' with others, such as Alexander's Chief of Staff, Dick McCreery; and I was certain it was the right step. Moreover, I felt I knew Montgomery well enough not to propose it in public. Auchinleck had opened himself to the advice of many and as a result his command had lacked not resolution but the coherence that is the hallmark of great generalship. In his determination to bring order into chaos and provide unmistakable leadership, Montgomery threatened at times to go the other way. As time went on I recognized more and more that it was my duty as his Chief of Staff, not only to see that his orders were carried out effectively—which was something any self-respecting executive could do—but to see that his virtues did not become his vices.

This may well sound boastful—a quality not in keeping with

a good Chief of Staff. However I do not mean it to be. The events of those fateful years lie more than thirty years in the past, and Montgomery himself is no longer alive. I do not think it will diminish his greatness to define the nature of our relationship; indeed I feel it a matter of historical importance that I should do so. When Montgomery later forced the British Army, as CIGS, to adopt the Chief-of-Staff system, it was objected that such relationships are by nature personal and individual, and might not always work successfully in practice : in a word, that they are best kept voluntary, at the discretion of the commander. It is an argument that possesses much truth, and to ignore the essentially individual character of such a relationship is to blind oneself to reality.

Let me illustrate my point. At the height of the Battle of Alamein I spoke privately to Montgomery about new intelligence from our 'Y' services that indicated a change in enemy dispositions. By altering the direction of our proposed thrust we would take maximum advantage of the new situation. Montgomery didn't take long to agree. He not only altered the plan, as commander; it became, in his own mind, his *own* decision, his *own* proposal, and was referred to as such in his diaries. In the same way, during the battle of Mareth, I suggested an alteration in the conduct of the battle in private, and summoned the Corps Commanders in readiness. As soon as he acknowledged the soundness of my reasoning, Montgomery made his decision : a decision which then became his own, in his diaries, in his campaign account and in his *Memoirs*! I did not feel any disappointment at this subsequent failure to give credit; I recognized from the beginning that this was the way his mind, his personality, worked. How many times would he turn down an idea one day, and announce to me the following morning : 'Now, Freddie, I've been thinking about X and I have decided to do the following . . .'! Such appropriation of ideas and designs is the very basis of command—at least the appropriation of the best ideas. It was my task, as I saw it, to know my Chief, to know how his mind worked so well that I could happily deputize for him in his absence, either in the field or at the conferences he so hated to attend; to know him so well that I might sense when to put forward a suggestion and when to bide my time; when to wake him or let him sleep. If there are those who feel this to be an idle or inconsequential matter, let me instance what happened when such an approach was not adopted.

No sooner was 'Supercharge', the final thrust, achieved at the Battle of Alamein than Air Marshal Tedder, Air C-in-C in the Middle East, began to champ at the bit. He had seen chance after chance squandered in the desert during his time there, and had rather an airman's view of the fluid battle, so that he could never understand why we British were so slow on the ground. Thinking of his elite flying crews, he could not perceive the realities of army life. Ignoring the feeble performance of the RAF in strafing Rommel's retreating Afrika Korps, he now dispatched a signal to Montgomery stressing the importance of sending a mobile force across the Cyrenaican bulge to cut Rommel off. If anything decided Montgomery not to pursue such a possibility— at least in strength—it was this meddling airman's presumptuous message. How much wiser to have visited Montgomery, congratulated him on his great victory, questioned him about the RAF's performance from the army's point of view, asked his needs and in privacy conversed about Montgomery's future proposals! Yet Tedder never learned his lesson—and caused a lasting rift in inter-Allied relations in the summer of 1944 by carping about Montgomery's slow Normandy performance behind his back (indeed urging his replacement) on the very eve of the greatest single victory of the war to date!

I could cite a hundred other examples like this. There is no use pretending that genius is common; it is not, and is often complex, difficult, even obnoxious. At Eighth Army HQ, and later that of 21st Army Group, we learned to live with Montgomery's 'vices' as the necessary counterpoint to his military distinction. Just as he was capable of unbelievable consideration towards others (such as the letters he would write to hospitalized subordinates, old colleagues or simple correspondents at the very height of battle), so too he could be guilty of meanness and cruelty. His vanity—inflamed by the manner in which, after Alamein, he became a household name—was coupled with strange humility at times; and his rigid obstinacy sometimes gave way to extraordinary realism. He referred to himself and me in his *Memoirs* as opposites, claiming that I was highly strung and lived on my nerves. But this wasn't altogether a true assessment: for as Bernard Shaw himself recognized, Montgomery's distinctiveness was his very tension. He was often impulsive and failed to consider the consequences of his actions, wounding people unnecessarily—even maliciously—as though he could not get rid of this tension in any other way. As with Hore-Belisha, my job became as much one of diplomacy as of military direction—particularly once our American allies came into his orbit. Though he demanded absolute loyalty himself and hated intriguers of any sort, he was undoubtedly given to this vice himself—a habit which almost cost him his command at the end of 1944 when Eisenhower lost patience with his capricious subordinate.

There is no doubt in my mind that fame on the one hand and widowerhood on the other made for an uncomfortable existence. Together with the strain of war—for Montgomery held field command in battle or pre-battle conditions without pause from August 1942 to the end of hostilities—these stresses were formidable, and it is remarkable that Montgomery survived them. Patton, the only other claimant to the title of genius on the Allied side during the war, did not survive the pressure, and was twice removed from his command as a result.

To be Chief of Staff in such circumstances was not easy; and if Montgomery's health did not suffer, my own did. I made mistakes myself, some of them costly—such as the failure to make clear to my Chief the paramount importance of securing the sea approaches to Antwerp as early as possible; but such mistakes were, I hope, compensated for by the march of our victories from Alamein to the Sangro and from Normandy to the Baltic. Had anyone suggested such a victorious advance in the early summer of 1942 they would have been sent for medical attention!

As Chief of Staff I complemented my Chief, one might say; and Montgomery had no hesitation in asking the King to knight me from the field of battle in Normandy, 1944. Thereafter came the crushing victory at Falaise, and the flight of the Germans to the gates of their homeland. It was from this moment, in the autumn of 1944, that my greatest difficulties began.

The extent of the Allied victory in Normandy was frankly never envisaged at the planning stage; indeed, without Hitler's help it would probably not have been achieved. We had assumed that the Germans, once they saw the red light in Normandy, would withdraw to the Seine; beyond that we had no formal intentions.

This was unfortunate, for there now arose a controversy over the correct form of strategy that would smoulder to the very last days of the war—and beyond. Here was the very greatest dilemma for me. As Chief of Staff, 21st Army Group, I had worked hand-in-hand with the American Army Group Staff which formed under Omar Bradley in August 1944. In this manner I was perhaps more acquainted with the tensions and problems of inter-Allied staffs than Montgomery was, as temporary Commander-in-Chief of Land Forces. Montgomery saw the future direction of the war through the lens of Commander-in-Chief; I saw it through the humbler eyes of the Chief of Staff at Main HQ.

Montgomery favoured a single northern thrust. It was not disloyalty on my part to see that such a proposal, however militarily attractive, was simply not feasible in the context of an Anglo-American offensive in which the British were facing north and the Americans east! It meant negating Patton's powerful thrust towards the Saar, making General Devers' southern army redundant and bringing a reluctant Bradley under the British umbrella. Montgomery offered to serve under Bradley; but as Bradley did not favour such a single thrust towards Germany this was something of an empty gesture.

If Hitler had played into our hands in Normandy, we now played into his. Montgomery was correct in his prognosis: no individual group was strong enough on its own to force its way across the Rhine that year. Yet having predicted what would happen, Montgomery attempted to defy his own logic in the most ambitious Allied operation of the war: the airborne assault on Arnhem.

I wish I could say, as Montgomery's Chief of Staff, that I wholeheartedly endorsed this imaginative undertaking. The Airborne Corps wanted it—were terrified of the war ending without their being employed again, and being condemned to watch while their transport planes were used as supply craft. Eisenhower was eager; he was undoubtedly anxious to prove himself a capable commander in the field now that he had usurped Montgomery's title. The army was willing—it was indeed heady after the great dash from Normandy virtually to the Dutch border in a matter of days.

Unfortunately I cannot say that I did support this, Montgomery's supposed master-stroke; but as I was in hospital in Aldershot I was powerless to dissuade him. I attempted to, on the telephone; for there were too many ifs in the plan and Prince Bernhard was warning, from his intelligence network in Holland, that German armoured units were stationed there. However, to my telephone warnings Montgomery merely replied, 'You are too far away, Freddie, and don't know what's going on!'

I suppose it is a moot point whether, had my health permitted me to be present at the time, I could have stopped Montgomery from committing this folly. Certainly it demonstrates how important it was to Montgomery's genius to have a Chief of Staff intimate enough to curb his impetuosities without causing him to lose face. From Aldershot, linked only by a telephone, I could do nothing; moreover, with the growth of our armies and Montgomery's increasing habit of living forward at his Tac HQ and spurning conferences, there was no one with sufficient weight or trust to act on my behalf. The loyalty and admiration he inspired now worked against him, encouraging him to a series of blunders. The corridor to be punched up to Nijmegen and Arnhem was too narrow, and the airborne landing too far from the Arnhem bridge. Urquhart was not the right choice to command the British landing, and increasingly adverse intelligence was ignored. The prize was a planner's dream—the cutting-off of Holland, with its V-bomb sites, from Germany, and a launching point for the invasion of the German plains; yet the assumptions were a planner's nightmare. What the operation demonstrated was what Montgomery had always proclaimed: that the Germans were masters of defence, and the bright ideas of people like Tedder were not only romantic but dangerous.

One might have thought that the loss of the Battle of Arnhem might have cooled Montgomery's ardour for his single northern thrust; but though he was subdued in the field (it was touch and go whether we could hold our bridgehead now) he waged an incessant war on Eisenhower to be given control of all the northern groups of armies—supported, I am sorry to say, by various colleagues at the War Office in London. His estrangement from Eisenhower, whom he only saw a handful of times that autumn, was ridiculous; and when he showed me 'Simbo' Simpson's petty account of the high living at Allied HQ in Versailles I flung it on the floor. Things were very cool between us after that!

If Eisenhower was wrong to remain so distanced from the front, then Montgomery was equally at fault to isolate himself in his ivory tower at Tac HQ amidst the adulation of his personal staff and the troops. The way in which he refused to attend conferences but always sent me instead became a joke at Supreme HQ. Montgomery hated conferences, it is true : hated having direct questions fired at him. It was a strange fact in one who was so brilliant at firing questions himself; but there it was. Thus time and again I was sent to represent him, which I did to the best of my ability; but all the time wishing, for the sake of Allied solidarity, that Montgomery was not so cussed.

Eventually, in December 1944, the Germans caught us napping in the Ardennes and Montgomery came back into his element. Yet so much had he distanced himself from Eisenhower, Bradley and Patton that his cool and efficient reaction was bitterly resented. Despite my urging, he refused to commit sizeable British units in counter-attack, so that the Americans were bound to feel they had won the eventual struggle while Montgomery was taking the kudos. Moreover, instead of allowing the question of command of the northern sector to decide itself by force of circumstances—Montgomery had been given command of two American armies for the battle—he used the breakthrough as a vindication of his endless campaign to be given complete command in the north and priority in supplies. This was tantamount to insubordination—especially as Montgomery was applying pressure via Simpson and Alan Brooke at the War Office. Eisenhower in the end prepared a signal to General Marshall, offering to resign.

I have described elsewhere how I sensed something amiss and journeyed—without informing Montgomery of the purpose—to SHAEF (Supreme Headquarters Allied Expeditionary Force) headquarters to ascertain the truth. After a personal interview with Ike I was able to stay the signal and race back to Montgomery's Tac HQ with the draft of an abject apology in my pocket. Montgomery sent it; but had I not gone to SHAEF I fear it would have been Monty's scalp that would have been rendered up, not Ike's.

Montgomery was grateful to me at the time; but neither in his diary nor in his *Memoirs* did he reveal that the reparation had been my own doing—indeed he claimed to have sent me himself to Paris to find out the 'form' !

Was it this that sowed the seeds of Montgomery's later re-pudiation of me? I continued as his Chief of Staff to the end of the war, after Monty's doctor had given me a final 'lease of life' until May 1945, by which date I would have to resign my position on grounds of health and undertake a full convalescence. This was disappointing to me professionally, since I had been told that Churchill had put me down as Deputy Military Governor of the British Zone of Germany; but doctor's orders were orders, and I left 21st Army Group following the German surrender.

By the middle of summer I was safely ensconced in the lakes of Scotland when the phone rang and I was ordered to London. Montgomery had heard he was to be the next Chief of the Imperial General Staff; and he wanted me as his Vice. But as I had no proper experience of the War Office apart from my term with Hore Belisha, I was to go immediately as Director of Military Intelligence to work myself in for six months. I explained that I was not fit and disliked the post, but would agree if it were con-sidered necessary before becoming VCIGS: the No. 2 post in the British Army. I was still only forty-five; it was an honour indeed.

Doctor's orders were cancelled, and I duly took up my post as DMI in Whitehall. I frankly despised the atmosphere of feverish anxiety over future appointments, and was known as John the Baptist preparing the ground for my Chief. Yet when Mont-gomery finally appeared—he did not choose me as his Vice.

Chapter Two

On Civvy Street—Rhodesia

The real reasons why Montgomery decided not to take me on as VCIGS at the beginning of 1946 can be left until later in this book. For the moment, however, let us ascribe it to ill-health—on which grounds I left England with my wife and daughter for three months' sick-leave in February 1946: destination Cannes.

A kind friend—Aly Khan—had lent me a little villa right on the front and a few yards from the Palm Beach Casino, and on arrival we found that a very nice couple had been engaged to look after us. It was wonderful to see this lovely part of the world again. Luckily the war had done little to mar its beauty. But better things were in store for us.

The War Office, showing the greatest understanding, agreed to supply me with British Army rations for five persons from their depot at Marseilles. This may not sound a tremendous privilege, but it was. Food in the South of France was most difficult to get at that time, and it was also very expensive. I remember working it out one day with Eddie Dissat who owned the Montana Hotel, which was being used as a leave centre for the RAF. He figured that on the black market the rations we received per day would have been worth over £40. A lorry used to call two or three times a week and I found that we were on an extremely distinguished ration list, as the Windsors who were living at their delightful château at Cap d'Antibes, were also entitled to draw army rations. He was still a General in the British Army. And it was through this housekeeping tie-up that I first made the Duchess's acquaintance.

The Montana Hotel was also on the ration list, and Eddie Dissat and I became firm friends and remain so till this day. He fought in the French Resistance and received the OBE a few

19

years ago, which made him immensely proud, and only recently was awarded the Legion of Honour. He has always been a great admirer of the British and there were few famous Royal Air Force officers of that time who didn't know him.

In addition to the War Office's efforts to help us, I received extraordinarily kind treatment from the Americans. On the first evening after our arrival, two large American cars drove up to the villa, and out of one stepped a wartime colleague of mine, 'Texas' Stevens. He had been for some time in charge of BUCO which was the organization responsible for operating the cross-Channel movement service to Normandy. He now had an enviable job as officer commanding the American Leave Centre in Nice, and was living in a fine suite at the Negresco Hotel—all found by 'Uncle Sam'. He had received instructions from Eisenhower to see what he could do to make my leave enjoyable, and he certainly carried out his instructions to the letter. In the first place he announced, after we had drunk to our happy reunion, that the other motor car, a Cadillac, was at my disposal, and what was more, there were two French drivers. This was a wonderful concession as petrol in France was strictly rationed. Then out of the boot came a couple of cases of drink, together with a selection of American tinned foods. I was also given authority to use the American Forces' Canteen. We were really in clover, and in addition to all this, Stevens entertained us frequently at his apartment in Nice. These were wonderful days and I found myself relaxing sufficiently to start on my first book, *Operation Victory*. In fact most of it was written during the three months we spent in Cannes.

Never having written a book before I tried to discipline myself and on most mornings would sit under the trees in the front garden and scribble away until a servant appeared about 1 o'clock with a large dry Martini. Generally this would be the signal to down tools for the day, but sometimes when I felt in the mood, I'd continue in the afternoon.

The butler would ask me what I would like for lunch, and it was always beautifully served. Aly had come under my responsibilities in Cairo when I was DMI, Middle East. Undoubtedly he was a playboy but a most attractive one, and the women fell for him right and left. He was, as everyone knows, a great gambler and used to take the bank at baccarat at the

Mohammed Ali Club in Cairo. He usually took my money. His main job was to look after those Arabs of his sect who lived in Syria, etc. He did this very well indeed.

Whilst in Cannes I began to think seriously about my future. Did I want to serve on in the army? I had reconciled myself to missing out on the appointment of VCIGS, which would have meant being in the No. 2 position in the army at the age of forty-six. I expected that I would be given a pretty good post when I regained my health. But having served so close to Montgomery for three hectic years of war, I realized I should find it difficult to settle down to post-war soldiering. Also from pre-war experience I knew that when generals served out their time, their brains often became rather addled and with rare exceptions they were unfitted to start up in some other walk of life. By the time my sick leave drew to a close I had begun to think of retiring from the army altogether.

Finally these halcyon days at Cannes came to an end, and we all returned to London. Soon afterwards I had to go into hospital once again for an operation, and that finally decided me to ask to be allowed to resign. This was not an easy matter, because regular soldiers were not permitted to do so because of the serious world situation that still existed. So I asked Montgomery for his help. At first he was not in favour, but after I explained my reasons he agreed to take up my case. Before long I received news that approval had been given. Faced with this new situation, I had to decide what to do, as my financial resources were insufficient to live a life of ease with no earned income coming in. I therefore started looking around for a job. In this I was singularly unsuccessful. I was offered the appointment of Public Relations Officer to the Federation of British Industries, but turned this down because I didn't feel qualified for such a role.

Then I was told that the Parliamentary constituency of Blackpool North, a safe Conservative seat, would like me to consider becoming their candidate. But nothing came of this. Shortly afterwards I was invited to see the Secretary of State for the Colonies, with a view to being considered for the Governorship of Southern Rhodesia. Such an appointment would have meant security and a comfortable life for a few years, but at the end of the usual five-year tour of duty, one would again be faced with

the problem of future employment. During the subsequent interview it became clear to me as well that there was another candidate who was being favourably considered for the post. He was
General Sir John Kennedy, who during much of the war had
been Director of Military Operations at the War Office. His wife,
Kitty, was a most experienced social worker and so it was clear
they would make a good team. I was therefore not surprised when
I heard that John Kennedy had been appointed. It turned out
to be an excellent selection as he proved a most successful and
popular Governor, and his wife was a tower of strength.

With nothing worthwhile appearing on the horizon, I began
to think of making a fresh start overseas. I had no important ties
in England and my wife came from Australia, so there was
nothing in particular that made necessary our living in England.
I first considered Australia, and with this in view I asked their
Minister of Immigration, who was on a visit to London, to come
for a drink one evening. From all he said Australia sounded like a
land of great opportunity, although with the massive immigration
programme there would be a housing shortage and other dis-
advantages. Besides this I sensed that my wife was not all that
keen on returning to live there. I then thought of Southern
Africa—Rhodesia or South Africa. In 1926 I had set out to
join that splendid Colonial Corps, the King's African Rifles, and
the ship had called at several South African ports on its way to
Beira, from where I set out for Nyasaland where I was to be
stationed. I was very much attracted by the country and its
friendly people. It was a country rich in resources and there were
obviously considerable opportunities and, at that time, no serious
racial problem existed. While I was trying to make up my mind,
I received news from a young Rhodesian officer who had served
on the Eighth Army staff; his name was Bob Long. He was a
first-class chap and later became head of the Rhodesian armed
forces. He suggested I should come to Rhodesia, and described
the life there in glowing terms. I more or less knew what to
expect because I had spent five years in the old colonial days in
central Africa. He also told me that their Prime Minister, that
magnificent character Sir Godfrey Huggins, later Lord Malvern,
would welcome me as an immigrant. So after a lot of thought
I finally decided to take the plunge and leave England for
Rhodesia.

During the weeks before we sailed I was extremely busy polishing up the galley proofs of my book *Operation Victory*. This is always a very exciting period for any author, particularly when it is his first book. The question of a title came up, and with the help of my friend Alan Moorehead, I decided on *Operation Victory*, which seemed to meet the case.

I had hardly got over one operation when I had to face another. Archie MacIndoe took me into his hospital at East Grinstead to give me a new nose—mine had been badly smashed in an accident on the way to Cannes. Archie specialized in operating on pilots and others of the RAF who had been badly disfigured by burns and other injuries. He did fantastic work and was dedicated to this type of surgery, and the way he would give a man a new face by expert grafting was almost miraculous. What is more, he did not let things rest there as he used to look after these unfortunate men after they left his hospital, helping them to find appropriate employment, etc. He was one of the most warm-hearted men I have ever met and it was all too sad that he died just before he was to become the President of the Royal College of Surgeons. He richly deserved this honour. On leaving the hospital I asked him for my account, but he scoffed at the idea and refused to take any fee, saying that this was the least he could do.

His kindness was illustrated by the following incident. Shortly after my operation, the first Alamein Reunion was due to take place at the Albert Hall. He knew how disappointed I was at not being able to attend and have the opportunity of meeting my old wartime friends again. About lunch-time on the day the function was to take place he came into my ward and with a kindly smile on his face said, 'Freddie, you're going to the Albert Hall tonight, but only for a short time.' He then explained that I was to be taken up on a stretcher in an ambulance and that he and his charming theatre sister would accompany me. On our arrival I was carried into Monty's box and allowed to stay there for about an hour, while the formal part of the proceedings took place, and was then removed to the ambulance and driven back to East Grinstead. I shall never forget this extremely kind act.

I realized that I was taking considerable risks in leaving the army, as my financial resources were rather limited, and it was

23

therefore important that I should find some employment within the next few months. In those days one's army pension was very small and compared most unfavourably with those given by industrial companies. Today however far better terms are enjoyed by officers when they retire. Besides the modest capital I possessed, I was due to receive a reasonable sum for my book *Operation Victory.* However I was not unduly worried as I was still comparatively young and had sufficient confidence in my ability to earn a living.

We sailed from Liverpool in October and took nearly three weeks to reach Cape Town. It was really an uneventful voyage but nonetheless a pleasant and relaxing period. We met a number of ex-servicemen and South Africans who were returning home, delighted to be going back to their beautiful country.

During the journey I tried to clear my mind as to how I would organize my life in the immediate future. Colonel Sir Ellis Robins who was then the resident director of the British South Africa Company, with his headquarters in Salisbury, had kindly offered to put up our family on arrival and until we found other accommodation. He was a remarkable and charming man. He had served during the war and took a leading part in the public life of Rhodesia. There was no good cause which he did not support, in fact you could call him the uncrowned king, as the BSA Company was extremely powerful in that country. A few years later he was recalled to London to become the head of BSA and was given a peerage before he died. There was no honour more deserved.

Friends of ours in the Cape had engaged a white nurse for my daughter and so these essential matters of accommodation and a nanny were taken care of. We had reserved rooms at the comfortable, well run Mount Nelson Hotel in Cape Town. During the South African War this hotel had become quite famous. It was here that the wives of officers fighting the Boers stayed and of course it was used by soldiers when on leave.

As for my plans in Rhodesia, I was determined to start by having a complete holiday, and as for a job I vowed I would try to learn the hard way if I entered industry.

I was thrilled when the ship entered Table Bay, a beautiful place I hadn't seen since 1931. Summer was in full swing and the surrounding countryside looked most inviting. We were met at the quayside by a wartime colleague 'Bomber' Harris, who had settled in Cape Town after his retirement. He couldn't have been kinder and we spent a few enjoyable days in the Cape, driving around, racing, and attending parties. I felt that I had made a good decision to come out to this part of the world. Although cars were in short supply, I bought a new American car with the help of Bomber Harris and arranged for it to be railed to Rhodesia.

When I left for the north my wife decided to stay behind until I'd got things organized in Salisbury. I left alone on a train which, like all trains in those days, was not air-conditioned. It proved to be a hot, tedious journey; taking about two and a half days.

Sir Ellis met me when I arrived at the Rhodesian capital and we drove to his charming, comfortable, and well staffed house, June Hill, in the suburbs. He told me I could stay as long as I liked. However before long I rented a small furnished suburban house for two or three months and my family joined me, spending a few days at June Hill before moving in. The car had also arrived and so we were ready to settle down and enjoy the freedom of a country like Rhodesia. After the rationing and restrictions in England, the abundance in this country was a joy. There was no problem about meat or petrol and the shops were well stocked. The people were as friendly then as they are today, and we were overwhelmed by their hospitality.

I saw a great deal of Bob Long, who had been on my staff in the desert, was now a Colonel, and was shortly to become a Brigadier. He and his wife did all in their power to make us feel at home. Bob asked me to give a series of lectures to the armed forces, and so I gave them accounts of the various campaigns in which I had taken part. I enjoyed this contact with the services immensely. I was also asked to make numerous speeches on all sorts of subjects, some of which I knew little about.

I met the Prime Minister on a number of occasions and was very much impressed by this sensible and straightforward man. He explained to me his ideas on 'the Native policy' as it was called. He was then advocating the two pyramid policy, which in effect was a form of apartheid, i.e., the white and black races remaining separated but with no restriction to their progress within their own ranks (a policy that is a bit out of date). In later years he changed his views, as everyone is entitled to do as the world progresses—particularly politicians!

The Prime Minister had a fine sense of humour and I remember an amusing incident which I witnessed when listening to a debate in the local House of Parliament. Sir Godfrey Huggins was very deaf and used a pair of earphones. When not in use the earphones were hung up on a stand in front of his chair. On this occasion the Leader of the Opposition, I think his name was Schmidt, got up to make a slashing attack on the Government. It was clear that Schmidt was well prepared and eager to ram home his views. After his opening remarks, which were pretty pungent, the Prime Minister felt he had heard enough, and so with a laboured gesture and with a sweeping motion, he replaced the earphones on their stand. This must have been very disconcerting for the Leader of the Opposition, knowing that his speech was literally falling upon deaf ears.

I made friends with Roy Welensky who was then leader of his party in the Northern Rhodesian Assembly. He has always been an attractive and robust character and I took to him immediately, as we found we shared the same views. From being a prize-fighter and an engine driver, he rose to become a statesman of the highest order. It was a cruel blow to him when the Central African Federation, to which he was so dedicated, finally broke up.

Within about a couple of months of our arrival, General 'Bimbo' Dempsey arrived out and stayed with us. He was on his way to South Africa at the invitation of General Smuts. Dempsey, the self-effacing commander of the 2nd British Army under Montgomery, fulfilled his task with great distinction. It was a blow to many of us when he died at far too young an age. It was great fun to talk over our war days together in peaceful Rhodesia.

A couple of months after our arrival General Sir John and Lady Kennedy arrived to take over the Governorship. They were very kind to me and I helped Lady Kennedy with some of her activities. I remember on one occasion she asked me to try and sort out a problem the Government was having with the Coloured community. They were not keen on having a European representing them in government circles. I flew over to Bulawayo for a meeting with their leaders and soon found I was faced with quite a problem. One or two of them asked the very simple question, 'Why can't we represent ourselves when matters concerning our own people crop up?' At least two of them appeared to be very intelligent and I felt great sympathy with their views. As far as I can remember I failed to achieve the object of my mission. I reported to Government House and I really don't know what was the final outcome.

Early in the year proof copies of my book arrived in Salisbury and I made minor corrections that were needed. As the contract stood, my book was to be sold on a royalty basis, but a clause allowed me to change it to an outright sale up to ten days before the date of publication. I was ill in bed at the time and wasn't feeling very bright. As I read through the book I became more and more depressed, and formed the opinion that it would prove a flop. So I worked out the relative merits of the royalty agreement and an outright sale. I felt quite sure that my publishers would have difficulty selling the first edition alone, and as an outright sale would not attract any income tax, I might do better by changing the terms of the contract. This meant of course that I would only receive the 'advance on royalties', after which the book would belong to the publishers. So I cabled my literary agent and requested him to make the change. I received a reply strongly urging me to stick to the royalty agreement as both he and Hodder & Stoughton were confident the book would be a success. In spite of this advice I stuck to my view and so the agreement was changed to an outright sale.

In the event I made a mistake, for *Operation Victory* was a great success; seven editions at least were sold as well as a paperback version and two subsequent impressions. And so through lack of confidence in my first book I missed making a lot of money. To my surprise and delight *The Times* of London agreed to serialize the book, which I believe was the first time they had done such a thing. Instalments appeared in six consecutive editions and leaders were published on the first and last days.

My old wartime Chief was not slow to congratulate me— 'quite first-class' Field-Marshal Montgomery pronounced in a letter in February 1947 after reading the whole book. What he felt about my criticism of his single-thrust strategy in 1944 was, however, quite different.

It has always been my view that administratively it could have been done [he defended himself in his letter]. The real reason that Ike wouldn't do it was that it meant halting the right, i.e. the bulk of the Americans. He said that public opinion in America wouldn't stand it. I told him that victories win wars and not public opinion . . . the broad front strategy finally led us into the most frightful mess, involved a great waste of life and meant that the war had to go on to the summer of 1945. My plan involved a bold move; but the prize was terrific.

It was a clear emphatic justification—but then he had said the same thing about Arnhem, an operation I also disagreed with from the very beginning!

Six weeks later Monty wrote to me again—this time asking me not to

go into print again on the issue. You have seen what I say in Chapter Eleven of 'Normandy to the Baltic'; I gave my view of what were the two possible courses open; said which one I favoured and why; said what conditions were essential if my proposition was agreed; gave the Supreme Commander's decision; and then passed on. I indulged in no controversy. You opened the controversy in your book; Miles [Graham] replied: I remained silent as I always will.

What is the good of my Chief of Staff and my CAO (Chief Administrative Officer) having an argument in the Press over a matter which was the sole concern of Ike and myself? It is no good and can only make things awkward for Ike and me, who must remain silent.

Thereafter I did as the Field-Marshal bade me, and rested my case. However, as we shall see, neither Ike nor Monty did in the ensuing years—both of them remaining far from silent!

Of course Monty was in a difficult situation, being now the head of the British Army, a man of Whitehall and in constant combat with a government determined to reduce the army and close down our colonial obligations faster than Monty—or any soldier—felt feasible without bloodshed. In the event the millions killed in the partition of India and the historical débâcle in Palestine confirmed his worst fears—and in the ensuing years we both corresponded a great deal and met on numerous occasions when Monty would pour out his frustrations. 'There is trouble enough in the world without stirring up any more,' wrote the future author of *The Memoirs of Field-Marshal Montgomery* that April.

Chapter Three

Gemsbok Assignment

At four o'clock one afternoon, while holidaying at the Leopards Rock Hotel near Umtali, I was called to the phone and to my great surprise heard a wartime friend of mine, David Stirling. He told me he had flown specially over from Salisbury to see me and asked whether it would be possible for me to drive to Umtali straight away as he had something of great importance to discuss and had to return to the Rhodesian capital in daylight. Whatever the particular purpose of his visit might be, I agreed to set out immediately.

The Stirlings are an attractive family, all three brothers possessing considerable personalities. David, the youngest, did exceptionally well in the war until he was captured in 1943. He was a very brave man. In spite of being held in maximum security prison camps, he nevertheless made several epic attempts at escape. He formed a 'private army' in the Western Desert called the Special Air Service Brigade and for a time, before Rommel and the German troops arrived in strength, he brought off some outstanding *coups* behind the enemy's lines. He was brave, resourceful and enthusiastic. He was also a tremendous optimist. Bill, the head of the family, who lives at Keir, the large Stirling estate in Scotland, was a commando leader during the war. Keir is a wonderful place and I have had many happy times there, and the shooting is exceptionally good. Every bird is to be found there, from grouse to geese; and Bill is the best host I've ever come across. He is a first-class and generous shot and always makes us lesser marksmen feel at ease. The third brother, Peter, was in the diplomatic service; but during the last few years has made a great success of a business enterprise in Persia.

Now back to David. I arrived at the appointed rendezvous in

Umtali and we greeted each other with enthusiasm. He had brought someone else with him, a young man in the 'city' called de Villiers (later Sir Charles de Villiers, a very successful banker, and chairman of the British Steel Corporation). As there was no time to lose, David ordered drinks and we got down to business. He explained that he had organized a London Syndicate who wished to get into Africa, and their first objective was Rhodesia. The idea was to acquire companies, enlarge them and gradually expand into any field that appeared attractive. He mentioned the old company, Willoughby's, which owned large tracts of land but was very inactive as far as development was concerned. Their main operation consisted of selling off portions of their vast estates. The aim was in some way to get control of Willoughby's and then use it as a base for greater acquisitions. As for the immediate purchasing or starting up of smaller companies, the expression used was 'in order to obtain a vehicle for entry into Africa'. I might add I heard this expression used a great deal in the future. I was given some details of what had already been done, and the men he had already recruited. After these preliminaries David told me they wanted me to become chairman of the 'Gemsbok Corporation', which was the name they had chosen for their enterprise—a gemsbok being a beautiful African antelope.

I was naturally surprised at this proposal because I had no business experience whatsoever and in any case, as I pointed out, I wanted to continue my long holiday. I asked about the financial side—what resources were available and where the money was coming from. He explained that the main backers were the Harley Drayton group, Philip Dunn (the *News of the World*) and certain other prominent concerns. He went on to say that he had held discussions with the Anglo-Transvaal Group in Johannesburg and claimed he had been promised £200,000 or more from them. My immediate reaction was to wonder why these people should have entrusted so much cash to David who really had little practical experience in the business world, although he possessed many qualities, such as leadership. However, there it was, and I was faced with a very difficult decision.

I was told that my role would not be full-time, but it was important they should have to lead the organization someone who had a reasonable reputation and who lived in Southern Africa. We argued for some time and in the end I gave my very tentative agreement, reserving the right to change my mind after I had had time to examine what it was all about and meet the various people concerned. I admit I didn't feel altogether happy as I knew so little about finance and industry, but David's enthusiasm and forceful advocacy were very difficult to resist. There was one angle which fitted into my own approach to my new life : this would certainly be an opportunity of learning the hard way.

On completion of my holiday I returned to the capital and shortly afterwards moved into a furnished house in Baines Avenue, Salisbury, which had just the amount of accommodation I required.

Soon afterwards I was invited by Field-Marshal Jan Smuts to pay an official visit to the Union, to be shown the country and give a series of lectures on the war to the various military headquarters. I was delighted, as I very much wanted to have a good look at this fast-developing state. A government aircraft was sent to Salisbury and I flew off to Johannesburg, very excited at the prospect.

Before I was invited to South Africa, I had received a charming letter from Smuts, in his own hand, enclosing a copy of one written to him by Bedell Smith who was then American Ambassador in Moscow. I reproduce them here.

Cape Town
5. III. '47

My dear General,

Very belatedly I have received a letter from Bedell Smith of which I send you a copy as you may like to have it. It is a wonderful testimonial.

If I could perhaps be of any assistance to you you will know how glad I should be to be helpful.

With kind regards,
Ever yours sincerely,
J. C. SMUTS

EMBASSY OF THE
UNITED STATES OF AMERICA
MOSCOW, November 20, 1946
My dear Field Marshal:

When we last talked in Paris, I spoke to you about Freddy de Guingand, and you were good enough to say that you would keep him in mind. I believe he has already left England for Southern Rhodesia, having missed an appointment to a governorship by a matter of days.

General de Guingand is the best staff officer I have ever seen regardless of nationality; and if our American military theories are correct, he would have been equally good as a commander. He would fill with great ability any position under government in which the Union of South Africa might see fit to place him, and I do not know of any man in whom I have more confidence and for whom I have greater affection. Since I know he will never approach you or anyone else on his own behalf, I am taking the liberty of reminding you of his availability.

Faithfully your friend,

Bedell Smith.

Field Marshal Rt. Hon. Jan C. Smuts, P.C., C.H.
United Nations General Assembly,
NEW YORK, N.Y.

I was very moved by Bedell's thoughtfulness. To have sent such a letter when he must have been extremely busy was a demonstration of what a good friend he was.

I travelled round the country in great style and comfort and met a number of interesting people, including several wartime friends. Whilst in the Transvaal I was looked after by General Everard Poole, who was then Deputy Chief of Staff and had been nominated to succeed General Sir Pierre van Ryneveld as Chief of Staff. He was a fine soldier and had commanded the 6th SA Armoured Division which fought so well in Italy. Unfortunately he never became Chief of Staff because in 1948 the National Party came to power and another general was appointed in his place. Poole was given a diplomatic appointment and he remained serving South Africa in many posts overseas, very nearly up to the time of his death.

Examining my changed programme, I found I had some time

on my hands and so, on the second night in Johannesburg, I rang up the chairman of the Anglo-Transvaal Group and asked whether I could come and see him. He sent a car after dinner to take me to his house. There I met Bob Hersov and his partner 'Slip' Menell. We talked late into the night. These two tycoons had built a considerable empire in the mining and industrial world.

My main object was to check up on what David Stirling had told me about the group's agreement to invest several hundred thousand pounds in the 'Gemsbok Corporation'. I told them that I couldn't believe that such astute businessmen would be prepared to hand over large sums of money to people who had little financial or business experience, unless some specific proposition had been thoroughly investigated. I found that my views were confirmed, and they explained they had never agreed to a *carte blanche* financial contribution, but were quite prepared to invest in any attractive proposition provided they approved the venture after adequate examination. They were however very interested in expanding into Rhodesia. Having cleared up this point we talked about Rhodesia and its future, about the war and a number of other things. I enjoyed my evening very much and liked these two successful South Africans.

The next morning after breakfast I received a telephone call from Slip Menell asking me to lunch at the Carlton Hotel. I naturally expected that they had had perhaps second thoughts about Gemsbok and so looked forward to our meeting with hopeful anticipation.

We met in a private room and after a dry martini we settled down to lunch. For some time the conversation was pretty general but towards the end Bob Hersov looked across at Slip and said, 'Well, you'd better shoot.' It was then that I got the shock of my life, for he told me they would like me to join the Anglo-Vaal board. This was of course entirely unexpected and after so brief an acquaintance I found it difficult to understand. I replied politely saying I was very flattered by the invitation but wondered what real help I could be to them as I had no knowledge of finance or mining. My days in the army had perhaps given me some administrative experience and I was used to certain types of negotiation at top level, but that was about all. They both assured me that they felt I would prove of value to the group and added that I would be happy and secure. I replied that I was

34

more or less committed to Gemsbok and I didn't feel I could let David Stirling down. This they assured me would not prove a stumbling block, as I could devote a certain amount of time to this company's affairs.

I had to think very quickly. Here was an opportunity of landing a worthwhile job of a permanent nature, and yet I kept reminding myself that I had vowed to learn the hard way. To accept would be the easy way out. To gain time I asked Slip what the remuneration would be and in reply he said, 'May I ask you what is your present income?' My answer came quickly: 'I can't see what that has to do with it, for I presume you will pay me what you think I'm worth.' So an annual salary was mentioned, together with certain fringe benefits, such as a house and a car. Although it sounded quite generous to me I hesitated for a while, trying to make up my mind. I suppose my hesitation made them think that their offer was too small and the suggested salary was immediately increased by a very reasonable margin. After some discussion I made up my mind to stick to my original plan and I politely refused the offer. I must admit I wondered whether I was not being a fool to turn down such an attractive opportunity. I liked these two men very much, for they were obviously highly intelligent and warm-hearted. We parted on friendly terms expressing the hope that we would meet again.

It was not long after I arrived back in Salisbury that Slip Menell telephoned me and put forward a proposition. He asked me whether I would be prepared to go to the United States on a special mission for his group. All he could tell me on the phone was that I would probably be away for three weeks and that I should arrive in Johannesburg a few days before the date of departure, to be briefed. I told him I would let him know within a couple of days. I had never visited America before and this would give me the opportunity to do so without expense. There was also the possibility of selling my book in the USA, for sales in North America were not covered by the outright sales agreement which I had made with my publisher. I decided in favour of the proposal, rang up Slip Menell and we fixed up appropriate dates. He very kindly invited my wife to visit Johannesburg with me and we were put up in a spacious suite in the Langham Hotel.

I spent two or three days being briefed. The Anglo-Vaal Group, in association with an American chemical engineer called Dobie Keith, proposed setting up an oil-from-coal plant in the Transvaal. The continuous process of gasifying the coal and converting it into a synthetic spirit had never yet been done. South Africa had an abundance of cheap low-grade coal and as Johannesburg was some 400 miles from the nearest port, the petrol produced in the area would therefore enjoy artificial protection as the cost of bringing petrol from the coast was considerable. A licence had been applied for, but the Government wished to satisfy itself as to the feasibility, both technically and financially, of the operation before they were prepared to issue one. It had therefore been arranged that two or three experts from the Government would proceed to America and in conjunction with Anglo-Vaal's chemical engineer, Frank Melvill and myself, would carry out a thorough investigation. My job therefore was to 'bear-lead' the team, open doors, and generally report on our enquiries. After three days of intensive study of the problems involved, I had a fair idea of what I was supposed to do.

I was booked on the inaugural direct flight from Johannesburg to New York by Pan-American Airways. We touched down at the Azores and arrived that same evening in New York, where I was met by Leonard Buck who was associated with Anglo-Vaal. He took me along to the Plaza Hotel where a truly magnificent suite had been reserved. I wasn't used to such treatment, but nevertheless I enjoyed it.

The next day Frank Melvill and the Government contingent met to discuss our plans. Leonard Buck took me out to his beautiful home in Far Hills, New Jersey for the weekend, where I met his family. He had two very pretty teenage daughters, one of whom had the distinction, so she claimed, of introducing John Kennedy to his future wife Jacqueline. His other daughter married Johnny Pine, who also lived in these parts. Leonard was a perfectionist. He had a world-renowned rock garden which was a pleasure to gaze upon. Later he took up breeding trotting horses and over the years has owned one or two champions. Whilst there I lunched with Charlie Scribner, the publisher, and from this contact I managed to sell my book, which I considered a great achievement.

I don't think the book sold very well in the United States but

I was very proud of the testimonials that Eisenhower and General Bradley agreed could be printed on the dust cover. This is what they wrote:

GENERAL DWIGHT D. EISENHOWER, in a letter to Major-General de Guingand:
'To my regret I've found no time to read more than a very few of the war narratives so far written. But for yours I simply had to make an exception not only because of your war-time post as Chief of Staff of the British Eighth Army in Africa and Italy and later of the British 21st Army Group in Europe, but because of your personal standing among all your associates as one of the truly brilliant officers of the Allied Armies in Europe. The presumption of authenticity which automatically attaches to your story by reason of your war-time vantage point of broad responsibility is confirmed, for me, by the accuracy with which you have reported incidents of which I had personal knowledge.

'I found your story most readable and of great interest; I'm glad you wrote it.'

GENERAL OMAR N. BRADLEY:
'Because staff officers are almost always anonymous, it is unlikely that Major-General Sir Francis de Guingand will ever be properly credited for his share in winning the war. I knew him not only as one of Britain's most brilliant soldiers, but as a friend and ally whose patience, modesty and understanding helped us to forge the allied armies into a single fighting machine. Somewhere in almost every critical allied decision of the war in Europe you will find the anonymous but masterful handwork of this British soldier.'

I also met Dobie Keith, who lived at Far Hills, and he described to me in simple language the process which he had developed.

The next two weeks were very hectic. I stayed with Eisenhower who was then Chief of Staff of the US Army at his house in Virginia, outside Washington; held discussions with the government department which handled the oil industry, talked to the military experts on the strategic value of establishing an oil-from-coal plant in South Africa; held discussions with certain oil companies and many other authorities. We also visited an experimental synthetic oil plant. After a rather sticky start we all got along very well together and I think I can claim that my mission was a success.

It was on this occasion that, when I was staying with Eisenhower, there had been a lot of talk of 'Eisenhower for President', but he had consistently said that he was not interested. One evening when we were enjoying a highball, I asked him whether he was determined to refuse nomination then or in the future. Finally I said, 'Surely if you felt the American people really wanted you as their president, would you refuse them their wish?' After some thought he replied, 'Well, if you put it that way, perhaps I might have to change my mind, but I would have to agree with the party platform.'

I must mention an intriguing character whom I met in New York. He was Louis Marx who in those days was, I believe, the biggest toy manufacturer in the world. He was a very wealthy man and extremely generous. During the war he used to send plane loads of 'goodies' to Eisenhower and Bedell Smith, to be distributed to the forces: numerous boxes of cigars, cases of whisky and all sorts of other presents. I remember receiving a lovely box of cigars from Bedell, as I happened to be visiting him at the time a cargo arrived.

After the war Louis Marx played a significant part in Eisenhower's election campaign. I believe he thought of and produced those 'I like Ike' buttons that many people wore in their jackets. Bedell had written telling him that I was going to visit New York. When I arrived at my hotel I found flowers and a letter offering me anything I might wish for. He was very involved in the theatrical world and every day he would send me tickets for the latest shows. A Rolls Royce was placed at my disposal and he entertained me on a lavish scale.

For several years afterwards a large crate of toys would arrive in Johannesburg at Christmas-time by air. I became very popular amongst young people because of this. I'm sure he will not mind my telling the story of how he became engaged to be married. When visiting his office one day he introduced me to Barbara, whose particular job on his staff was the design and marketing of various articles for women's handbags. Not only was she most efficient but she was also extremely beautiful—strikingly so. She sometimes joined Louis and me when we went out to dinner. I sensed that there was a romance around the corner. One particular evening Louis invited me to dinner and the first night of the musical *Brigadoon*. I was told to meet him in the bar of a well known restaurant. When I arrived I found Louis leaning over the bar looking very disconsolate and sipping a cocktail. He hardly spoke when I arrived and merely signalled the barman to give me a drink. A little later I realized what had upset him, for in walked Barbara (she is now called Idela) with a well known male film star. They made up our party. During dinner the film star held the floor, which did little to improve Louis' mood. On arrival at the theatre the crowd soon recognized the film star and there was a lot of clapping. He sat with Barbara in one row and Louis and I sat together in the row behind.

At the interval Louis looked so miserable that I suggested we might leave and go back to his apartment for a drink, which we did. It wasn't long before my friend began to talk about his future. From what he said it was clear he was in love but couldn't make up his mind whether he should take the plunge. I had no hesitation in advising him to do so. I told him that I thought Barbara was a delightful girl and I felt sure she would make him very happy. This seemed to cheer him up, and in the early hours of the morning I left for my hotel. A very short time afterwards he asked Barbara to marry him, she accepted, and they became a very happy couple. He has three sons and I have a photograph hanging in my study showing a distinguished collection of military men, three of them with Louis' boys on their knees. They were the godfathers. The group consisted of General Marshall, General Eisenhower, General Arnold (USAF), General Bedell Smith and General Bradley. It would be difficult to find a more renowned collection of top brass!

A few years later I arrived in New York just before lunch and rang up Louis Marx to fix a meeting. With his usual warmth he said, 'You're just in time, Freddie; dine with me tonight and then we'll see the world heavyweight championship.' I was delighted, for we witnessed the Rocky Marciano fight from ringside seats.

Chapter Four

The Move to South Africa

Having carried out my task in America I wrote a long report and flew back to Johannesburg, where I called on Bob Hersov and Slip Menell. I think they were pleased with what had been accomplished and considered our mission would help to persuade the Government to issue Anglo-Vaal with a sole licence for embarking on this project. A few months later when I came to live in Johannesburg, I was asked to fly to Cape Town to see Smuts with a view to accelerating the issue of the licence. It was quite interesting to see how the great man worked. I explained that the delay in getting the licence was causing us embarrassment and told him that the group had spent a great deal of money on investigations. In his usual dictatorial way he replied, 'Yes, there is no need for further delay,' pressed a bell on his desk and asked one of his ministers to come and see him. When this gentleman arrived he said, 'Why hasn't this oil-from-coal licence been issued?' The minister made some sort of excuse, but Smuts cut him short and told him to issue it without delay.

This was agreed upon, but it wasn't the end of the story. The next problem was to raise the necessary finance. I think it was estimated that some £10 million would be required. But owing to the uncertainty of the new process and the fact that it would take at least four to five years before there would be any chance of receiving a return on capital, the raising of the necessary cash proved an insuperable problem. So in the end it became obvious that this was a project that could only be handled by the Government. Strategically it was most important and therefore it was only right that they should accept the responsibility. As I understood it, the licence was returned to the Government and Anglo-Vaal was reimbursed for all the expenses it had incurred. Many alterations were made in the process and the design of the plant, and the final cost rocketed to somewhere in the region of £50 million or more. A new township called Sasolberg had to be built not far from Vereeniging. This undertaking finally proved to be a great success and a new chemical industry complex has developed around the plant which has contributed towards the country's industrial expansion. Recently the plant has been enlarged considerably.

It was during this visit to Johannesburg that I met King George VI and Queen Elizabeth, who were visiting South Africa and staying at Government House in Pretoria. My wife and I received an invitation to spend Sunday with them—alone, as it turned out. As I have related elsewhere, the King asked me for a copy of my recently published book, *Operation Victory*, and the Queen said, 'The King, I'm sure, would like you to autograph it for him. But,' she added with a smile, 'I suggest you don't inscribe it as your Chief did his book, which he recently sent the King.'

I politely inquired what had been written, and as far as I can recollect it ran as follows:

Your Majesty,
I am sure you will find this book intensely interesting.
Montgomery of Alamein.

How wonderful to have Montgomery's superb confidence in his own achievements!

I once related this story to him and his reply was simple: 'What's wrong in that? They were interesting, weren't they?'

As David Stirling was in Johannesburg we had an opportunity of discussing Gemsbok affairs. I was still not altogether happy at the prospect of becoming its chairman. He wanted me to meet one of the men from the City of London who was involved in finding the money. His name was Erland d'Abo. I think he was an original member of the London syndicate. So a meeting was fixed in my suite at the Langham Hotel. D'Abo duly arrived and was most charming. The way he introduced himself amused me. Having shaken hands, he said, 'Well, General, I don't really know how to describe myself, but I would say that I am in the fortunate position of having an almost unlimited income!' I don't know what impression this was meant to produce, but at the time it left me quite cold. We discussed Gemsbok and he did his best to persuade me to agree, once and for all, to become its chairman. He assured me that I would be provided with all the help I needed; but even so it was only after a dinner party at the County Club that I finally accepted the appointment.

I think it was about this time that I was vetted by the powerful Anglo-American Corporation. A wartime colleague of mine, General Ken Ray, who had been Chief Engineer of the Eighth Army, had written me to say that this group was looking for a managing director and that he thought this might be a good job for me. It was arranged that I should lunch with Sir Ernest Oppenheimer, his son Harry, and one or two others. We had an excellent lunch at their offices and I found Sir Ernest an extremely colourful man. His successful rise to becoming the most important financial, mining and industrial figure in South Africa was an exciting story. I heard nothing more about the matter and it was obvious that I was not considered a suitable candidate. How right they were. With my lack of experience, I was quite unfitted for such a responsible executive post.

The Oppenheimers were very liberal-minded and Sir Ernest was always doing what he could for his workers. When the Free State mines were opened up, he wanted to build a large area of married quarters so more of them could live with their families. But I believe the project was forbidden by the Government. They no doubt felt that it would lead to demands for similar action in other areas.

Returning once again to Salisbury I immediately set about examining the Gemsbok assets. These had been acquired by David Stirling, the object being, as I have already said, to provide a 'vehicle for getting into Africa'. The companies were as follows: a small building concern which concentrated on houses because there was an acute shortage in the country; a drilling company for sinking boreholes—every farm and householder was in need of water; a transport company which operated bus services from Salisbury to various other towns. As roads were far from good, the bodies had to be made locally, and turned out to be of very poor quality. Another company had been formed to undertake estate work. Various other possibilities, such as chrome, were being looked into. A secretary/accountant had been engaged and the majority of the executives were ex-servicemen, all very good chaps but most, I'm afraid, with little previous business experience.

The more I probed the Gemsbok assets, the less I liked what I found, so I co-opted the services of an ex-bank manager who had been recommended to help me carry out an investigation. The report we produced was a pretty depressing document, and the main conclusion reached was that we would do well to dispose of the various companies and start afresh. In letters to our London principals I indicated my fears, but received comforting replies telling me that the necessary expert personnel would be sent out to due course. In any case I was asked to carry on until they paid a visit.

Eventually Erland d'Abo touched down in Salisbury *en route* for Johannesburg where he was to meet up with David Stirling. I met the aircraft, and asked Erland to sit in my car during the stop and read the report which I had prepared. It took him some time and at the end he expressed a certain amount of concern. He left saying he would be back in a few days. In point of fact he didn't arrive for nearly three weeks, and by then he had developed a robust approach to the Gemsbok companies. I guessed he had been influenced by David Stirling's confident and optimistic outlook. It wasn't altogether different from advising Wavell over the defence of Greece in 1941!

I then started to look round for other opportunities and heard from the manager of the Standard Bank that the executors of a deceased estate were prepared to sell a large plot of land called Mapelreign situated, in those days, on the outskirts of Salisbury. I think it was about 1,200 acres in size. The main drawback was the lack of water. There was no reticulated water system laid on and any attempts at drilling boreholes had met with failure due to the extremely hard rock which underlay the area. However Salisbury was expanding at a tremendous rate and it was obvious that the city would before long stretch out to encompass the Mapelreign Estate. Also a large dam, to be called McIlwaine, was to be constructed a few miles from the city. Therefore within a few years water would become available. The price asked for this land appeared very reasonable—I think it was in the neighbourhood of £45,000. So after consultation with our London associates I bought the land, being quite prepared to sit on it until water became available and demand for building-land in

43

the area developed. When I left Gemsbok just over a year later, I advised my successor to hold on to Mapelreign, for I was sure that we had a little gold mine there. Unfortunately it was sold far too soon at about double the price we paid. It might have been necessary in order to raise cash; but it was a pity. About four or five years later I was visiting Salisbury and asked the town planner what the estate would have been worth if we had held on to it. His reply was £1¼ million! We ventured into one other property deal and bought a large ranch in Northern Rhodesia near a place called Chobi. It cost about £30,000 and was sold I believe at a slight profit.

About this time several of the London partners came out and I met Harley Drayton for the first time. They were very helpful and I particularly took to Harley Drayton who was a very robust character. He arrived at Salisbury airport in a small chartered aircraft on a very hot day and stepped out of the plane wearing a bowler hat and carrying an umbrella. He certainly brought a City-of-London atmosphere to Rhodesia. Philip Dunn, who accompanied Drayton, couldn't have been more charming, but a problem arose with the *News of the World* people. One of the family, who I believed owned a controlling interest in this newspaper, flew out a month or two later to investigate their investment in Gemsbok. Having had a good look he decided it was not quite their 'cup of tea' and eventually pulled out. I couldn't blame him.

Shortly after this I visited Johannesburg again because we were negotiating the takeover of a construction company. We concluded the deal but it did not turn out too well. We tried to obtain partners and I can't recollect how it all ended. Because of this acquisition, and for other reasons, I was asked whether I would be prepared to shift my headquarters to Johannesburg. This I agreed to do. In October 1947 therefore I left Salisbury to live in South Africa, where I was to spend the next twenty-five years of my life.

On this visit I was once more approached by Bob Hersov and Slip Menell to join the Anglo-Vaal Group, and they made the offer even more attractive. I must admit I was sorely tempted, but in the end I again declined. We reached a compromise and I was asked to join several of their company boards. The fees were very generous and there were no executive responsibilities involved. I accepted with gratitude. Not only did I welcome a continued association with these two men whom I admired and considered my friends, but the additional income would increase my independence.

Bob Hersov was taken ill and died that year. This was a great blow to his many friends. He left a widow, Gertie, and two sons. They were a devoted family. Gertie is a charming woman whom I often meet on the golf course or across the bridge-table. Basil, the eldest son, is very able and is now chairman of Anglo-Vaal; he served in the Air Force for a couple of years. The death of Bob Hersov meant that Slip took over the chairmanship of the group and he had a long and successful period of office. He was a delightful companion with a keen sense of humour, and we developed a close friendship over the years. It was towards the end of 1969 that the group discovered a very large and valuable copper deposit in the Northern Cape. He was as excited as a small boy and one day took me into his office saying, 'Freddie, at long last I've hit the jackpot,' and then proceeded to tell me all about it. It was an unkind stroke of fate that he died a year or so later.

During 1948 I was asked to join two other boards—General Mining Industries and Keir & Cawder, a company started up by Bill Stirling. Towards the end of 1947 I was asked to dine with Gordon Richdale who was then one of the top executives of the 'Corner House' group. On the way home he suggested that his group might like me to join them. However I had made my decision and indicated that I couldn't accept. Later Gordon joined Charlie Engelhard's empire in the USA on most attractive terms, but, after his five-year period of office, returned to South Africa where he is still very active and successful. He wrote a delightful book which he called *The Sunlit Years*. In it he described his life from the days when he worked in the Bank of England. He asked me to write the foreword to his book, which I did.

I finally moved to Johannesburg in October 1947, but from this time onwards I became increasingly unhappy; none of our companies appeared to be living up to forecasts and we were still very short of first-class personnel. There was a premium upon top management in Rhodesia and South Africa, and so I hoped that the early promises of assistance would be forthcoming.

Sometime in 1948 I decided that the best thing for me to do was to get out of Gemsbok. I discussed this step with David Stirling, who I found was equally unhappy, and so I approached Francis Ridsdale who looked after some of Harley Drayton's interests in South Africa, and told him that I thought it would be better for all concerned if I left. He was very nice about it, but he evidently found it a bit difficult to disguise his satisfaction. There was no attempt to press me to stay on and in due course matters were arranged for my departure and I was given a year's salary by way of compensation. Having made the break I felt very relieved. I had learnt quite a lot the hard way, which I knew would prove useful to me in the future, and I was reasonably satisfied with my own judgement. I had from the start proposed that we should dispose of the original assets, had purchased two properties which could have proved very profitable. This doesn't mean however that someone else with much more experience than I had would not have made a better job of it.

I certainly didn't regret my decision to leave England—whence came a series of depressing letters from my old Chief. In fact at one point during this period he thought the situation there was so bleak he might actually be called upon to 'take steps'! 'If the thing goes sky high I may have to play a part : and would do so,' he assured me; adding that he considered I was 'needed in Africa, and indeed you are destined for great things in that continent.' We met when he came to Rhodesia in December 1947—and after I had given him a paper on the responsibilities of Britain towards African development he promised to 'make things hum when I get home'. A Cabinet meeting was duly arranged at 10, Downing Street to discuss Montgomery's African findings—and Monty wrote from the Channel Islands to tell me of it.

Creech Jones hated it and wrote a counter-blast. Bevin and Stafford Cripps agreed with it. It was decided to send Marquand out to investigate the whole matter, and he came to see me before he left. He is out with you now, I think; he is quite a decent chap, but he is not a big enough man I fear. Having launched the V2 rocket I pulled out and have been busy ever since on Army matters and on trying to get the Chiefs of Staff to really achieve something instead of being merely a debating society. This is, I fear, almost impossible.

Tedder is utterly ineffective; Cunningham's mentality is of the Boer War; Hollis is generally ill or tight; and A. V. Alexander is utterly and completely useless as Minister of Defence. There is only one hope for us and that is to have a 'Chief of Staff Armed Forces', who will be an independent chairman of the Chiefs of Staff Committee, and who will advise the Minister what to do and will make him give decisions.

Chapter Five

The Bicycle Business

About the time I resigned from Gemsbok I had been asked by both Anglo-Transvaal and General Mining Industries to take over the chair of a company called The Ace Cycle and Engineering Company Limited. The former two companies owned a controlling shareholding in Ace and as I was a director of each, I had to say 'yes'. I understood that all was not well with this company, so I looked on the invitation as a challenge. As it turned out, it affected the whole of my future industrial life.

Sir George Albu was the chairman of General Mining and also of its subsidiary, General Mining Industries; and Eddie Menell, Slip Menell's brother, was a director of ATI. The latter was also a director of General Mining Industries. All a bit complicated, but the connection is important.

Ace Cycles had a factory out at Springs, some thirty-five miles from Johannesburg, and its object was to make bicycles, as at the time none were made in South Africa. They were all imported. The company had acquired a certain amount of machinery but had nowhere nearly reached the production stage.

I attended my first board meeting and was duly elected to the chair. I can't say I was much impressed with what I saw and heard. The next thing was to go out to Springs and examine the factory and meet the works personnel. Eddie Menell came along with me and it soon became apparent that the company had little hope of producing a machine, because most of the components had to be imported and there was a world shortage of these. Also know-how was generally lacking, although they did have an executive from the Enfield Cycle Company, who possessed some practical knowledge of the industry. His name was Hobbis. As large sums of money had to be paid out each week to cover salaries and wages and nothing was coming in, it was only a matter of time before the company would become insolvent and the shareholders lose all their money. So I soon realized that I had been given a pretty hard nut to crack.

I decided that I had to start by doing two things. First to re-constitute the board, and secondly try to get some tie-up with an overseas company which knew something about bicycles. In due course I held a board meeting and asked all the directors to place their resignations in my hands. This was not a very popular move, but most of them agreed to do so. I think there were two who wrote to me saying they couldn't see their way to obliging. I then had to warn them that the only course open to me would be to call an extraordinary meeting of shareholders, and as we had the controlling shareholding, we would have no difficulty in appoint-ing a new board of directors. This threat did the trick. I kept the ex-chairman, Eddie Menell, and one other, and brought in one or two new men. Having cleared the decks at board level I then concentrated on the factory. The managing director left with a golden handshake, and Hobbis was appointed general manager. The factory was capable of making very little of a bicycle. We had a plant for producing frames and handlebars. We could do some enamelling, a certain amount of plating, tyres could be bought locally, but most of the other components had to be im-ported. There was a certain amount of plant which could in time be used for making components—that is, when we could procure the right materials and possessed the technical know-how. It stuck out a mile that no time should be lost in getting in touch with some substantial manufacturer overseas.

With this end in view, I wrote to a very old friend of mine, Sir Geoffrey Burton, who was then managing director of the Birm-ingham Small Arms Company. Amongst many other things, they made bicycles in a small way. I explained my predicament, and asked him to advise me. I received a quick reply and he strongly recommended that I should contact Ivan Stedeford (later Sir Ivan), the chairman and managing director of Tube Investments, the large British engineering group. He claimed that they were at that time the largest people in the cycle business. As Geoffrey Burton knew Stedeford quite well, I wrote and asked him to find out if he would be prepared to see me if I flew to London. I received a favourable response, so Eddie Menell and I set out to

49

see what we could do to salvage Ace Cycles. We stayed at the Savoy Hotel and at the appointed time we walked round to the TI offices, which were situated virtually next door.

This was my first meeting with Ivan Stedeford. I, of course, knew of his reputation. From the time he had become chairman he had expanded his group and it had progressively become more and more successful. He was of the old Birmingham school of industrial leaders: tough, prepared to make decisions and maintain the power in his own hands. He was tenacious, and possessed the courage that is so necessary in an industrial leader.

After the usual preliminaries, we described the object of our visit and I made a great deal of the fast-growing industrial scene in South Africa, and how the Government were determined to encourage local manufacture whenever this was practical. As our foreign exchange position was not healthy, import control had been introduced so Government policy was to help new industries by granting a measure of protection. Because of all this I was convinced that the time was ripe for TI to take the plunge and start making bicycles in the Union. He listened attentively and admitted that he knew little about the country, although his group did a good export business. But because of an agreement entered into with Stewart & Lloyds, they were prevented from making steel tubes in South Africa. Why such an agreement was ever made I never understood, as when I joined TI I found that they had got little in return for that except for some cash, which they really didn't need. I think it was the old story of looking on the Union only as a mining country. It was not appreciated that the war had given a tremendous impetus to industry because of the artificial protection which war conditions provided.

It was clear to me that Stedeford saw the force of my arguments and indicated that he was interested. He asked for details of the Ace Cycle company, which we gave him, but he made the point that the present export sales from his British factories to South Africa were considerable, and his bicycles were sold at very attractive prices. There was such a world shortage that they had more or less to ration exports. Before we left, Stedeford asked Eddie and me to a dinner party so that we could meet some of his directors, including the heads of his cycle companies. Before this, however, we had another meeting at which we got as far as drafting heads of agreement, setting out a broad basis for a deal. I had come to a firm determination that whatever agreement was concluded with TI or any other company, I would get our shareholders their money back, and I made this point from the start.

The dinner was a pleasant social affair and we liked the TI directors whom we met. The talk was pretty general but from odd bits of conversation I had, it was clear that the heads of the major cycle companies, Arthur Chamberlain and Jim Boultridge, were not very keen about the proposed deal. One couldn't blame them because at the moment they were making a killing from their export trade with South Africa. The next day our talks drew to a close and Stedeford told us he would give the matter some thought and would then write to me. We left London not too optimistic about the ultimate results of our visit.

Stedeford's letter duly arrived and confirmed my worst fears, because he asked to be allowed to send out a team of experts to examine the factory. This was a perfectly reasonable request but would undoubtedly result in their finding the cupboard very bare. I cabled back agreement, and out they came, spending a few days carrying out their task. I guessed what their conclusions would be. Before long I received a very friendly letter from Ivan Stedeford saying they had given our proposals a great deal of thought but had decided that the time was not yet ripe for such a move. Later when I joined TI I read the report and it stated that we would never be able to make bicycles and that in any case TI would only have to wait a few months for the company to go bust and then the factory could be bought at a knock-down figure.

Faced with a crisis on our hands, we had to decide what to do next. We were in a terribly weak position unless we could produce some bicycles. So it really became a choice between liquidating the company or producing the machines, at whatever cost, so that we had something to attract some outside interest. Eddie and I talked it over and decided we would at least go down fighting. On examining the various orders that had been placed with TI for components, I found that deliveries had been very sporadic and there were many letters explaining reasons for non-delivery, etc. The result was that the modest collection of components which we had accumulated were nowhere nearly balanced, and this prevented us from going into production, even in a small way. It certainly looked as if TI were not going out of their way to put us on our feet. But who could blame them!

This was a time for drastic action; we cancelled all orders placed with TI, because I was fed up with the unreliability of this source of supply. It might also make them think we were throwing in the sponge. How wrong they would have been if this was the interpretation they put on our action, for we now sent Hobbis, our general manager, on an overseas tour to buy 60,000 sets of the various components and accessories which we were lacking. He went all over Europe; to the back streets in Birmingham, to France, Belgium, Holland, Germany and elsewhere; and he succeeded in purchasing our requirements. He did a fine job. Now we could at least start making some cycles and so morale all round improved, although we knew that we were far from being out of the wood.

Laboriously the bicycles came off the line, and we started to market them. We could only produce one model in varying sizes. They cost us £12 each to make and we had to sell them at £7 in order to be competitive. So from the strictly commercial point of view it wasn't a very attractive operation! We encountered another obstacle in the wholesale trade. These people represented various overseas manufacturers and therefore were not very pleased with the idea of a local cycle industry. Bicycles were in such short supply that they had no difficulty in getting rid of all they could import and of course they had a wide choice of models —all shapes and sizes. They were also worried that, once local production could cater for the home market, we might be tempted to cut them out and sell direct to the retailer. Because of all this we didn't find willing buyers, and one has to admit that the quality of our machines was not at this stage up to their imported counterparts. Then one day a government tender was published for the supply of cycles for the Defence Department. This was a must, at whatever cost. In most government tenders the locally made product was given a 15% to 20% price advantage and so we put in a quote which we knew would be less than any a wholesaler could live with by supplying the imported article. We got the contract and we made the most of it from the publicity angle; but the snag was we lost several pounds on every bicycle we sold.

I wasted no time in writing to Geoffrey Burton telling him that we were now in business and had recently won a Defence Department contract for several hundred machines. I suggested that at some convenient opportunity he might convey this information to Ivan Stedeford. Not long afterwards I received a letter from the chairman of TI informing me that he had decided to pay a visit to South Africa with one of his co-directors, Peter Carew. He looked forward to renewing our acquaintanceship and asked whether I would let him have a look at our factory in Springs. I replied saying I looked forward to meeting him again and he was welcome to visit Ace Cycles.

Reading my *Rand Daily Mail* one morning, I noticed that space had been devoted to the arrival of a prominent British industrialist, Mr Ivan Stedeford, the chairman and managing director of Tube Investments. There was the usual hullabaloo accompanying such visits. I took no notice and waited for developments. Sure enough, in a couple of days Stedeford was on the phone saying that he had been in Johannesburg for the last two days. I made no comment but just waited. He then asked if he and his colleague could visit Springs. A date was fixed and it was agreed that they would lunch with me, after which I would take them out to see the factory.

We were very active between this phone call and the day of the visit. I went out and discussed the matter with Hobbis. It was agreed that no bicycles would be dispatched until the afternoon Stedeford was to arrive, and all possible activity was to be concentrated during the hours of the visit. Hobbis in his enthusiasm placed various components which had been bought overseas in the trays of machines which had still not been brought into operation, either because we didn't yet know how to operate them or because of a shortage of skilled labour. After a pleasant lunch we drove out to the factory and I was astonished at the activity to be seen on every side. The various departments looked very busy and numbers of bicycles were being loaded into delivery vans. It certainly looked most impressive. I naturally didn't mention that this great endeavour was costing us about £5 a bicycle.

During our tour I could see that Stedeford was duly impressed and I even overheard him make a very enlightening remark to Peter Carew such as, 'This is extraordinary, Peter; our people came back and reported that they would never make a cycle.' This gave me a very comforting feeling. The whole display reminded me very much of the sort of thing that happened in the army when one was trying to impress an inspecting general. At the right moment I suggested we should adjourn to the board-room for a cup of tea, and on the way Stedeford took me aside and said, 'You know, Sir Francis, I think perhaps we should start talking again about TI buying out your company.' This was music to my ears, but I decided to play it cool and made some such remark as, 'Oh, it's a bit late now just as we are getting into our stride. Having been awarded a government contract has helped a lot.' However I didn't slam the door and offered to have a chat about it in due course.

The next day Peter Carew asked me to lunch and I agreed to see whether we could work out something—in fact, hold meet-ings to try and reach a basis for agreement. He also said they thought it was about time that TI had some sort of set-up in South Africa and that the first thing for them to do would be to find a suitable representative. I wondered whether he was throw-ing a fly in my direction but could not be sure. The next day we started our meetings and at the outset I made my point that if we sold out I wanted the existing shareholders to get their money back. For some days we worked away and finally produced some very tentative heads of agreement, but we were a long way from solving the financial implications, as we repeatedly turned down various offers that were made. In the end Stedeford said he must return to England but promised to send out one of his executive directors to carry on the negotiations. The evening before his departure he asked me along to his hotel for a drink, and we went through the heads of agreement and both initialled them. Before he passed a copy over for me to study he said, 'You'll notice that I have added an additional clause,' and there at the end written in his own handwriting was a proviso that I should remain chairman and managing director of Ace Cycles and also become TI's representative in South Africa. This of course suited me very well, for having resigned from Gemsbok I only had a few directorships to bring in an income.

I therefore agreed and we discussed the salary and possible directions in which TI might branch out in this country. It was proposed that after a final agreement had been reached, I should visit England in order to learn something about the group. Before we parted he asked me if there was anything he could do to help and I suggested his secretary, whom he had brought out with him, should be transferred to my staff. I had been much impressed by her ability and I felt it important to have someone who knew the TI Group so well. I was delighted when he agreed to this, telling me that she rather wanted to marry and settle down in South Africa. She has been a tower of strength and I think is still working for the company. Her name was Ann Carter.

It was about this time that I was associated with two professional men in Johannesburg who became very good friends of mine, and who have helped me a great deal over the years. In the army one was meant to know something about the arms other than one's own, e.g., artillery, tanks, engineers, signals etc.; and at the staff college we were taught to handle all arms of the service. Nevertheless I was firmly wedded to the principle of making use of the expert, and I considered this was just as necessary in business. Arthur Aiken, a wartime gunner, was a distinguished accountant and besides other things was chairman of Barclays Bank in South Africa for a number of years. He is one of those rare people who, however busy they may be, are always ready to help one with any problem. I really don't know what I would have done without his shrewd advice on a number of occasions. The other 'expert' was Charles Friedman, a member of an important firm of lawyers. He was originally briefed by TI and from that day onwards he has advised them concerning all legal matters because of his great experience in the business world, and in a number of other spheres as well. I was indeed fortunate to have expert advice from these two men so readily available. They saved me from doing something stupid on a number of occasions.

Soon after Stedeford's departure a TI director called Norman Lancaster arrived to help work out a satisfactory solution. We had long and difficult meetings, some of which were acrimonious. On one occasion we were gathered together in Sir George Albu's office—Norman Lancaster, George Albu, Eddie Menell and myself—when discussion reached crisis point and in fact Lancaster told us the negotiations were off and that there was little point in meeting again. He then dashed out of the room. We sat and looked at each other wondering what was to happen next. It was really a desperate situation. We decided to think things over and meet again the next morning. We descended in the lift and stood

55

chatting on the pavement waiting for Sir George's chauffeur to bring round his car from the garage. When it arrived he got in and just as he was moving off turned to me and said, 'I know what I'll do, Freddie, I'll have a talk with father this evening and see what he advises we should do.' He then drove away. It suddenly struck me that this was a very odd remark, as I knew that George's father had died some years before. So I turned to Eddie and asked him what he meant. Eddie smilingly explained that Sir George was a spiritualist and claimed that at seances he sometimes got in touch with his father. So we waited to hear what advice would come from another world.

The next morning we met again in George's office and he told us he had been successful in 'getting in touch with father', who had advised us to continue the negotiations as this would be in our best interests. Later on that day Lancaster rang up to say he would like to have another meeting with us. The TI director was in a very different frame of mind and was most conciliatory, and then proceeded to work out on a piece of paper a new scheme for satisfying our insistence that our shareholders got out with little or no loss. He thought he could place a number of preference shares which would mean that the price they were prepared to pay for the equity would come very near the mark. A year or two later Stedeford told me he had been very angry when Lancaster had phoned him to report the impasse that had been reached. He instructed his colleague to continue the negotiations and produce a satisfactory agreement. His visit to our factory and perhaps the human spark ignited between us had saved the day.

1   2nd Lieutenant Francis de Guingand, commissioned in the 2nd battalion
Prince of Wales's Own West Yorkshire Regiment, 1919

2a Preparing the invasion of Sicily, 1943: Eighth Army HQ at Malta,
two days before sailing for Sicily. De Guingand is second from the left and
b   as Major-General, 21 Army Group, 1945

3a   Viscount Montgomery visits the Hercules Bicycle depot in Cape Town, South Africa and *b*   Viscount Montgomery 'has a puff' at one of the Rupert cigarette factories in South Africa

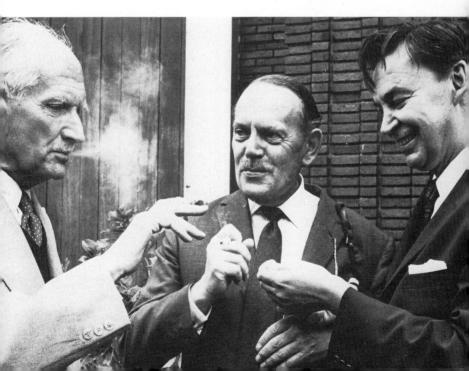

4 Three prominent South African industrialists: *a* 'Punch' Barlow, *b* Harry and Bridget Oppenheimer and *c* Anton Rupert

5 President Eisenhower with Mr and Mrs Louis Marx

6a Eisenhower's Reunion Dinner in London, 1959. De Guingand is nearest to the camera b Monty, on one of his many visits to South Africa – with Jim, de Guingand's labrador

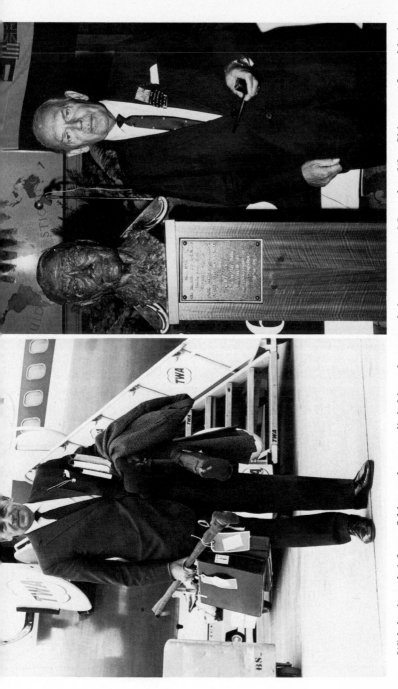

7a   With business briefcase, fishing rod, naturalist's binoculars – and the typescript of *Generals at War*, Chicago, 1962 and b   At the tenth anniversary of the founding of the South Africa Foundation, 1970, being presented with my bust

8a In the 'evening of life' in South Africa, 1970s and *b* Francis de Guingand with Rommel's old chief-of-staff, General Westphal, 1978

Chapter Six

Working for TI

In 1949 I promised to visit my in-laws in Australia whom I had never met before. My wife and daughter had already left by ship and I was now due to join them. I decided to catch a small Norwegian vessel which was leaving from Cape Town some time in June, direct for Adelaide.

I therefore asked Sir George and Eddie Menell to complete the negotiations, which now appeared to be on a set-fair course. During my voyage I received the welcome news that the agreement had been signed and so many weeks of toil and anxiety had been brought to a successful conclusion.

I flew to Brisbane to stay with my wife's parents and joined up with my family. I attended various ex-servicemen's functions and met some old friends. I visited the outback and had an amusing day's duck shooting. We flew to Sydney, but this coincided with the big coal strike and the great city was in darkness. In the Australia Hotel where we stayed, no lifts were working and the only hot food was cooked on primus stoves. However we enjoyed ourselves whilst in Australia, and I managed to fly to Canberra and spend a day with the Labour Prime Minister, Joseph Chifley. He was a fine Australian and had introduced an ambitious immigration scheme which opened up restrictions so that various nationals besides the British would be welcomed. A large number of Balts were coming in, and the big inflow of new Australians created great problems in respect of housing, education etc. Chifley realized that it was essential to increase the population of this great country as fast as was practicable. I spent a most interesting day with the Prime Minister. I was very impressed with Australia and one could feel that a great future was in store for this country. If I had been a young man, I would seriously have considered living there. Little did I know at the time that

I would be paying many more visits there during the years to come.

Several weeks had gone by since the agreement with TI had been signed, yet I had heard nothing from Stedeford and so became a little worried. Perhaps he had second thoughts about my joining the group. What about my proposed visit to England to learn something about their activities? I decided to fly to London and make contact. It was important that I should get things sorted out.

On arrival in London I learnt that the chairman was holidaying in the South of France with his family, so I flew to the Côte d'Azur, putting up at my favourite hotel in Cannes—the Majestic. The Stedeford family were staying in an hotel on Cap Martin, so I rang up and proposed paying him a visit. When shown to their suite I found he had damaged his knee very badly through falling into a manhole while going for a walk. He was in great pain and was flown back to London the next day. It gave me time however to clear up things, and after a few days holiday in Cannes, I arranged to report to TI's headquarters in London. I came to the conclusion that flying from Australia had been the correct decision.

I spent an interesting time with TI, meeting various executives, going round some of the many factories. I soon realized how much we had to learn and how necessary it would be to draw on their skilled personnel and technical experience. We also discussed what other operations we should start up in South Africa and it was arranged for the head of their electrical division to pay a visit with a view to starting up a Simplex company in this country. George Briggs, the Simplex chairman, was a flamboyant character and a most amusing companion. After a thorough look round he decided to buy a small company on the outskirts of Johannesburg which made switch gear and had a very old fashioned hand-foundry. Good business however was being done with the various mining groups, mainly because of the contacts established and the personality of the managing director. The idea was that we should use this company for getting Simplex Electric going, and then build a new modern factory with a mechanized foundry out at Springs, close to Ace Cycles.

I knew absolutely nothing about this industry but one or two experts were sent out from England. They were Don Nash for the production side, and John Morrison to handle marketing and sales. I was lucky as although neither of these men had had much executive experience, they were young and great fighters, and I can assure you we had to fight to avoid going bust. They both rose to positions of considerable responsibility. They possessed the qualities I liked—enthusiasm, loyalty and a desire to learn.

The day I arrived at the factory, to take it over officially, produced a dramatic turn of events. I had prepared what I thought was a fine speech which I made to all the staff and factory workers in a corner of the building. You know the sort of thing—how glad I was to have taken over such an excellent lot of chaps, how we were going places with all the latest know-how from the UK and how I was certain we would combine into a strong and successful team. I felt quite pleased with myself and appreciated the few handclaps when I had finished. I then returned to the office. Soon afterwards I was told that the two sales managers wished to see me. 'Certainly,' I said, as I expected they wanted to make some polite remarks and express their loyalty. I was shortly to receive a considerable shock. Closing the door, they informed me that they were leaving the company that very morning to take up other appointments. I have to admit that I was well and truly shaken. It turned out that the late managing director had started up a company of his own and, what was worse, had cast duplicate patterns of most of the castings which were in the greatest demand. The sales staff were also joining him. I didn't think it was quite playing the game, but I could do nothing about it. It would mean, of course, that our best customers would switch their business from our company to the new one, and the effect on our order book was catastrophic.

Then we were forced to go into the estate business. Housing was in such short supply that to be in a position to obtain good skilled labour, a house was a great attraction. So we bought a large plot of land on the outskirts of Springs and built thirty-five houses. This turned out to be a reasonable investment.

I will now turn once again to our cycle company which TI had taken over. All was not plain sailing as you will see. It so often happens in business that just when the way ahead seems clear, all sorts of snags crop up. One can never be complacent and must maintain a flexible outlook and be forever watchful.

I was sent out a young works manager who was not very

experienced, but he was keen and did his best. The Hercules Cycle Company loaned me their production director whose job was to lay out the factory and start the wheels rolling. He also advised on new plant which we should order and a host of other things. He was a very keen photographer and after a while began to spend a lot of his time in the game reserve taking pictures of animals. As I felt he had served his usefulness, I asked our head office to recall him.

At this stage we had to buy a large number of components from TI UK and often we found that many of them were of inferior quality. No doubt someone down the line thought this was an excellent opportunity of getting rid of their dud stock. This sometimes held up production. But nevertheless we progressed quite well.

Then the battle really started with the wholesalers who were still antagonistic, not without some reason, to local manufacture. To come face to face with them, I arranged a meeting one morning in a local cinema and I also invited members of the retail trade. It was a large gathering and I got up on the platform and gave an account of what we proposed to do, and expressed my confidence that with the full weight of TI behind us we would make a success of our undertaking. I was asked a lot of awkward questions. 'Might we sell direct to the trade from our factory?' 'What brands would we produce?' 'How many models?' 'What would the quality be like?' 'Would our prices be competitive?' I tried to answer them as best as I could but in some cases I could see they were not satisfied.

From then on manoeuvring took place by myself and the wholesalers with the Director of Import Control—Carl Borckenhagen. I was pressing for licences for the importation of plant and components, and the wholesalers for licences to bring in more complete bicycles. Borckenhagen behaved with great fairness, as he did in all his activities throughout his term of office. I also had to battle with the Board of Trade to obtain protection, and after very thorough investigations cycle imports were subject to a reasonable tariff. We had to promise to increase the local content of the bicycle as rapidly as possible and we made plans to do this. Within a year or two, we and the wholesalers buried the hatchet, when they were convinced that we could produce the goods. Their most powerful member was Johnny Hurwitz who had previously been the principal agent for the importation of TI cycles. However he finally became our greatest supporter.

Another irritation that came my way were the activities of a gentleman called Sir Edmund Crane. He had built up the very successful Hercules Cycle Company in Britain and soon after the war sold it for the nice price of £4,500,000 to TI. He was a really tough businessman and was not renowned for his generosity. The story is told of a farewell evening party he gave after selling out, where he had gathered together the men who had helped him make his fortune. There was a general atmosphere of anticipation and not unnaturally one or two were looking forward to a 'handout'. As the proceedings drew to a close Sir Edmund turned to his trusted old accountant who had helped him over many a hurdle and said, 'Oh—come down with me to my car.' Full of hope this faithful member of his staff accompanied him to the street. On arriving there Crane opened the boot of his car and brought out a brace of rabbits, which he had shot that afternoon. These were handed over with, 'I know you like rabbits, so I thought I'd give you these!'

Although Sir Edmund may have been a very tough operator in business, I had always found him generous in the social world and he had a very charming wife, who after his death married Lord Stanley.

After his deal with TI had been cleared up, he emigrated to South Africa and bought a large house situated in the hills behind Durban. He was of course most interested in TI's cycle factory at Springs and would pay periodic visits. I welcomed this because advice from a man who had made a fortune in the business was well worth having. I found, however, he had started up a correspondence with the chairman of TI and others, criticizing or making suggestions as to how the factory should be run, and I began to get the backwash. I was not prepared to have this sort of thing happen behind my back and went down to Durban and raised the issue with Crane. I told him that whilst I welcomed his advice, I could not tolerate what he had been doing. If he had suggestions or criticism then by all means he should raise them— *but with me.* I was in charge, and the responsibility for success or failure rested with me. I finished by saying, 'Now Ted, I'm sure you would have been the last one to allow such things to happen when you were head of Hercules.' His reaction was remarkably gentle. He said he saw the point and in future he would deal with me direct, and only if I agreed would he send a copy of any correspondence to Stedeford. From then onwards I made good use of Crane's advice. We became good friends and I have spent pleasant holidays cruising with him in his fine yacht in the Mediterranean.

Before leaving Sir Edmund, I must recount an incident which happened at his home. I had gone there to spend a night in order to discuss some of my problems. Soon after my arrival he said, 'You know your enamelling is bad—it's not hard, in fact it's soft.' I replied that I was surprised to hear this, as we had received no complaints. He then took me up to a room where he had one of our bicycles hanging up. Gripping one of the tubes of the frame with both hands he twisted each in opposite directions and then taking his hands away pointed to what looked like smeared enamel. The inference was that the enamel was so soft it was not stable when subject to pressure. I must admit I was surprised and worried, but then suddenly something rang a bell. Durban at that time of the year had a very humid climate. So I stepped up, took a silk handkerchief from my breast pocket, and gave the offending part of the enamelled tube a good rub and polish. Lo and behold, all the marks had disappeared. Now it was Ted Crane's turn to be puzzled. With a look of grim determination he went back to the bicycle and gripped the tube again and this time put every ounce of energy into the twisting process. He looked as if he might blow up, he became purple in the face. He then retreated, and once again I advanced with my silk handkerchief and the marks disappeared. Crane had the good grace to admit defeat and finally agreed that there was nothing wrong with the way we enamelled our bicycles. If I had not had that showdown about corresponding behind my back, I'm sure a very critical document would have been dispatched, without my knowledge, concerning the bad quality of our enamel.

In 1951 a bitter blow fell. Raleigh Industries, our major rivals, decided to build a factory outside Vereeniging. I realized immediately that if this happened, neither of us would make a profitable living, and Stedeford offered them participation in our Springs company. But they wished to go it alone. A magnificent factory was built and production started. The result was as anticipated; our profits, which were very good at that stage,

62

dropped considerably and Raleigh found the return on the capital they had invested was very small. After a year or two, when visiting England, I suggested to Stedeford that we should try to persuade Raleigh to merge with us in South Africa. He argued that I should see what could be done. I got to know the head of Raleigh—George Wilson—who was a charming and able Irishman. He was an expert fisherman and an excellent shot and during our discussions he invited me to fish on the Wye, and I also had an excellent day's shooting. To cut a long story short, eventually we concluded an agreement. We concentrated all production at Springs and took over some first-class members of their staff, including their works director. It was a complicated and difficult operation but in the end it proved a great success. Ever since then, the company has grown from strength to strength and TI have earned their capital investment back several times.

How wrong some people are who think that industry is a 'bit of cake'. There is never a dull moment and the battles and situations that crop up are just as challenging and exciting as are those experienced in the army in wartime.

Chapter Seven

Life in South Africa

In this chapter I propose to describe the life one led when I first arrived in South Africa, and how I spent my time outside business hours. In 1947 the country was experiencing a wave of prosperity. It had really done well out of the war due to the impetus that had been given to industry, and people and companies from overseas were rushing in to invest, and the stock market was booming. To someone coming from England with all the restrictions and rationing, it appeared a land of plenty. But of course our black workmen were paid very low wages.

I found the people whom I met particularly charming and hospitable; they were out to help a newcomer in every way. I know nowadays it is the fashion to criticize white South Africans and accuse them of avarice and inhuman feelings, but I can assure these critics that they are very wrong. Large numbers have extremely kind hearts and do all they can to help those less fortunate than themselves.

Suitable accommodation in Johannesburg was hard to find, but we managed to rent a large house with four acres of garden in the northern suburb of Illovo. We lived there for a few months under pretty uncomfortable conditions, because as it was temporary there was no use in ordering new curtains and carpets, and our furniture had to be gradually acquired. I remember in some of the bedrooms we used small packing cases with cloths over them for tables. It took us over a year before we found the house of our choice. It was charming and had a very nice garden and swimming pool, but before it was ready for occupation we were forced to live in various places—flats, hotels and rented houses. I suppose I was used to roughing it during nearly six years of war, but it was not a very easy life for my family.

A general election was held in 1948 and everyone took it as

a matter of course that Smuts's United Party would be returned to power. But just as in Britain, the first post-war election produced a great surprise. Britain repudiated Churchill, and in South Africa the United Party was defeated. That world statesman, Smuts, had taken things too much for granted. He had concentrated more on world problems than on the domestic scene. It seems almost incredible but he never once visited his own constituency, which he had held for many years, before the election took place. The result of the election came as a great shock to many people and the stock market reacted badly. But those conditions didn't last long, and there was so much energy and capital to be invested that the country's economic life bounded ahead. South Africa was, however, running into a balance of payments problem and before long the Government had to introduce import control. The National Government was now able to implement its policy of apartheid and separate development and it was only from the year 1948 that segregation, which up to that time had been an accepted way of life in the country, was made enforceable by law. This same party has been in power ever since.

During the post-war years I have witnessed a considerable industrial revolution taking place. When I first arrived the Bantu, or natives as they were then called, were flocking to the urban areas in search of work. They had no skills, no belongings and no houses. They spoke different languages and so in many cases the police could not communicate with them. They mostly lived as squatters in miserable shacks constructed on any spare land available. Most of them walked about in a pair of khaki shorts and a singlet, and few had boots and shoes. Their pay was grossly inadequate. It was a pathetic situation, but one must give the Government credit for tackling these problems in a prompt and decisive way. A crash programme was commenced for building large urban townships for the Bantu. This was a colossal undertaking as it involved the construction of thousands of houses, building railway communications to their places of work, sanitation, power and water supply. Some will say that the houses are very small, but they were infinitely better than anything they had been previously used to; which in most cases were mud huts with thatched roofs. Industry had to contribute large sums of money to help pay for all this and it was done by way of a 'site and services levy' based on the number of Africans a factory employed. The whole scheme turned out to be a great success. But of course there is no end to these problems and the authorities are continually being faced with new challenges.

As regards pay, I admit to having broken the rules, and I used to pay my top workmen sometimes twice what was usual and accepted by the white trade unions. I felt that one had to give these people a good target to aim for, and the policy certainly paid, for they worked harder and more efficiently than before.

There has been a great and general rise in wages of the workmen throughout industry, and this was mainly led by our own tobacco and wine groups. Dr Anton Rupert, who will figure later in this book, set an admirable example. One hopes however that this rise in wages doesn't run away with itself and make the various goods they produce uncompetitive.

Now let me turn to animals, of which I am a great lover. Africa, and South Africa in particular, is a wonderful place for wild animals of all sorts. I'll start with dogs.

I was delighted to be at long last in a home of my own and it meant that I could own dogs. I am a great dog-lover, and believe firmly in the old saying that 'a dog is man's best friend'. My first dog was a rather leggy black Labrador. Then I acquired my first dachshund. One gets very attached to these 'sausage dogs', but to our great grief he died of that horrible disease, hardpad. Then we bought two more dachshunds—one black and one brown. I called them Rommel and Keitel. They were a delightful couple and we all loved them very much. One day Keitel disappeared, and we were miserable and so was Rommel. As he had not returned for two days, I asked the gossip-column writer of the evening paper, *The Star*, to report that Keitel was missing. He gave the particulars and to my great excitement I received a phone call that same evening saying that the little dog had been found by a chemist in a southern suburb of Johannesburg. This was about ten miles away, so he must have been stolen and have managed to escape. I immediately drove out with Rommel and a great reunion took place. All went well until 1954, when one evening one of my servants was taking the two dogs for a walk round our block. A car, no doubt driven by a drunken driver, mounted the pavement and ran over both dogs. One was killed outright, and the other was so badly injured that we had to give him an injection to put him out of his misery. The driver of the car never stopped—I could have shot him. I then bought a delightful golden Labrador called Jim. He was a great character and a true friend. He had to be put down when he was twelve years old. I tried him out shooting but he was too enthusiastic, and when one shot a bird he would pounce on it and feathers would rise in clouds. In the end he had to be left behind which was sad, because he did enjoy these outings so.

Before leaving the subject of dogs I must tell the story of Jim and the dog parlour. I heard of a new dog parlour which was highly recommended. It was about a mile and a half from my house, and to reach it one had to travel through a rather complicated network of roads and through two shopping centres. Jim had to go there from time to time and came back looking rather sheepish and smelling like a tart. One day I came back to the house for lunch and was told by my servants that Jim was missing. A few minutes later the telephone rang and the owner of the dog parlour informed me that Jim had turned up there, and would I fetch him? I drove round and collected him, and was told he had scratched at the door and when it was opened, had walked straight in and entered one of the empty cages that the dogs were placed in whilst awaiting their turn, or to dry off after a shampoo. He apparently sat down and obviously enjoyed looking at the various animals being attended to on the table. But how he found his way there I have never understood, as he was always taken by car, and as I have already said, the route there was extremely complicated. Jim repeated this performance two or three times and finally gave it up. I suppose he looked on it as a dogs' club and loved going there to meet his friends and to hear a bit of gossip.

All my life I have been a very keen fisherman and shot; therefore I lost little time in exploring opportunities when I arrived in South Africa. I am not so keen on sea-fishing, but there is plenty of excellent trout-fishing available. There is a certain amount of private water, but a great deal of river and dam fishing is open to the public. Naturally it is not so good as it was in 'the old days', when it was truly superb, but provided one is prepared to go further afield it is still very good. I think the first trip I made was to Underberg which nestles at the foot of the Drakensberg Mountains on the Lesotho/Natal border. There is a beautiful river called the Umzimkulu, and many others within reach. This was in 1948, and trout running up to 3 lb. or 5 lb. were obtainable. I was never happier than when fishing far away from the towns, in the peace of the countryside with that wonderful African light. One could work out one's problems under such conditions.

I also joined a syndicate formed by a great friend of mine called John Voelker who held one of the top jobs in ICI in South Africa. He owned a small farm at a place called Dullstroom in the north-eastern Transvaal. Here there was a municipal dam through which a river ran and then flowed on through Voelker's land. He built another dam and we caught trout up to 5 lb. in weight. There were also several other good trout rivers within reach. John was a dear chap and the perfect fishing companion. He was a real countryman, a brilliant shot and an expert fisherman. Whenever we got tired of the bustle of business we used to drive up to Dullstroom, fish and relax. He was also a bird expert and he taught me a lot about those which were indigenous to that country. After he retired, he bought a small farm in Natal and lived there for a few years with his wife Jean, who was also a good fisherwoman; but he died about ten years ago. When I am casting my fly on one of those beautiful rivers, I think of John and hope that he may still be fishing in another world.

I sometimes stayed with Sir George Usher, the successful British industrialist who had bought a large farm and retired in South Africa. He had created two or three large lakes on his property and one evening after the sun set, I was present when a mutual friend, 'Digger' Farran, landed a 9 lb. brown trout and the local fishery officer checked its scales and proved that this magnificent fish was only three years and four months old. When you stock a dam in South Africa the initial growth is incredibly fast.

A great friend of mine—Punch Barlow—has a superb estate in the highlands of Natal, where there is some excellent trout fishing. He is one of the lucky men of this world, having taken over a comparatively small business from his father and built up probably the largest industrial empire in South Africa. He is a great sportsman, having captained Cambridge at both cricket and rugby, and in his day was a top polo player. In spite of all his success, he remains a very modest man. He has developed his farm to a high degree. There is a delightful private golf-course, and he has constructed three dams at different altitudes, which are all well stocked with trout, and fish up to 10 lb. have been taken. Punch is a bird-lover and has declared his estate a sanctuary so shooting is not permitted. It is a great joy to stay at Boschhoek, for besides there being such a choice of sport and entertainment, Kay, his gifted wife, provides you with all the creature comforts.

There is also a small stud farm and I have an old friend living there—an ex-racehorse of mine, called The Gen. He was kindly leased to me by Harry Oppenheimer and won me a number of races.

The shooting season is a short one and differs from province to province. Sometimes it may only last for six weeks to two months. There are plenty of guinea-fowl, various species of francolin and the largest are locally known as pheasants. There are also geese, duck and teal, and at certain times of year you can find snipe and quail. Many of the Afrikaans farmers are very happy to allow you to shoot on their farms, and I have always found them polite and kindly people. Then various friends of mine who owned farms would lay on well-organized shoots, when you might kill 150 guinea-fowl as well as a number of partridges. The farm labourers, particularly the small boys, thoroughly enjoy these shoots. Punch has also planted a great number of trees.

Probably the most enjoyable shoots I attended took place on the de Beers farm near Kimberley. It covers an enormous area, something like 100,000 acres. It was originally owned by Cecil John Rhodes. The old shooting box is still there and was built on good Scottish lines. In the early mornings we went for sand grouse, called Namaqua partridge. They fly into isolated patches of water and are great fun. Besides these birds there were usually plenty of guinea-fowl and partridges. And for those who like shooting buck there are thousands of springbok, many of which have to be shot each year. I've passed that stage, as I did so much shooting in my King's African Rifles days, so usually leave this to others. But the springbok are extremely good to eat.

The original game book is still there but the shooting in the old days was very much better than it is today. Drinking one's sundowners after a day in the veld, tales of the past are retold. One of the best yarns concerns a distinguished peer from England whom Rhodes was entertaining. He had unfortunately peppered a 'native' gun-boy rather badly in the back. As compensation he gave the unfortunate man a couple of shillings. But his friends pressed him to be more generous and so it was agreed that he should pay, I think it was a shilling, for each pellet that was recovered from the man's back. When the hospital report came in it turned out that over a hundred had been extracted, so he had to hand over something like a fiver, which in those days was a fortune to a poorly paid native.

During one of the de Beers' shoots one of the guns was a German whom we soon found out was an extremely dangerous shot. Whenever he lifted his gun you were wise to duck pretty smartly. Late one morning we were walking up guinea-fowl in some pretty rough country and I was next to the German. I suddenly heard a crashing through the bush in front of me. The next thing I knew I was lying on my back with my gun several yards away and some of my friends bending over me. My head felt very sore, so I put my hand up to explore for any damage and felt a large bump. My hand was covered with blood. As my mind cleared I shouted, 'That bugger has shot me!' But what had really happened was a female Kudu had taken fright and charged straight into me and thrown me on my back, and my head had hit a rock which had caused the damage.

Whilst writing about Kimberley, I can't resist telling two old stories about that legendary character, Barney Barnato. Rhodes had wanted to do a deal with him and part of the consideration was that he should be elected to the most exclusive Kimberley Club. It was certain that he would be blackballed, but Rhodes proposed him, and the day of the election arrived. When the ballot was over it was clear that many black balls had been placed in the box. At the appointed time for the checking of the votes, the secretary fetched the boxes and then on the way to his office tripped up and flung the boxes in front of him and all the balls, black and white, were scattered in every direction. Immediately Rhodes, who was chairman of the Club, announced that Barnato had been elected. All very peculiar!

The other story concerns a board meeting of a gold-mining

company. The chairman informed his co-directors that a certain borehole had produced very disappointing results. A short time after this announcement, Barney Barnato suddenly doubled up and let out powerful groans. Then getting up, he staggered to the door, but before he got there the chairman turned round and said, 'Come back, Barney, we'd *all* like to sell our shares before the Stock Exchange is informed.' And quite meekly Barney returned to his chair, apparently miraculously cured.

De Beers is of course the creation of the Oppenheimer family. When I first arrived in the country I came to know that remarkable man, Sir Ernest Oppenheimer, quite well. He had built up a great empire in the mining and industrial sector and was certainly the uncrowned king of the financial world. He had a finger in every pie. He must have been very tough in the old days in order to survive the struggle for power that went on amongst the great characters of the past, but now he had mellowed and was an extremely kindly and generous man. His son, Harry, was MP for Kimberley and was active in the business. When his father died he was faced with the problem—should he make politics his main occupation or run the Anglo-American Group?

After his father died Harry rang me up one day and asked to come to see me and ask my advice : What should he do? Which of the alternatives should he plump for? I had no hesitation in saying that I thought he had no choice—he must take over his father's group which would be a full-time job, as he owed this to the shareholders. I added that he couldn't possibly do both, and therefore a political life was out. He no doubt had asked others of his friends, but I suppose he wanted confirmation of the decision which I'm sure he had probably already made. As usual many people said that he would never match up to his father, but they were wrong. Under his astute and enlightened leadership Anglo-American Corporation increased its interests to become one of the most successful and powerful concerns in the world today. He spread it far and wide, in Africa, Canada, France, Australia and elsewhere, and I'm sure his father would have been proud of his son for what he has achieved.

Harry was educated at Oxford and all his life has had kindly and liberal views. He is a modest man, most accessible, and I'm sure, in fact I know, that those who work under him feel themselves lucky to have such an understanding and able 'boss'. He has always worried about South Africa's racial problems and felt that the United Party, of which he was a member, should review their policies. With some of his close parliamentary friends he worked out a new-look 'native' policy which aimed at advancing the status of the Africans and giving them some political say in the country's affairs. At one of the annual conventions of the party he presented his proposals, but the rank and file of the party turned them down. This was a great disappointment to him. Because of this turn of events a new party emerged which took the name of the Progressive Party. One of the main planks was to introduce a qualified vote.

This would of course have meant that many white voters would lose the franchise and it was therefore not a very popular proposal. A breakaway occurred and some five United Party members of Parliament joined the new Progressive Party. All but one lost their seats in the next general election. The sole representative elected to Parliament was a brilliant woman named Helen Suzman, who is still a member and fights the battle for her party from several seats, with great ability in the House. In the last election the party increased its membership. The opponents of the qualified vote believe that once given a vote, the African will never cease to agitate for the full franchise and this will lead to riots, disorder and eventual black domination. But unfortunately riots have recently occurred in spite of so qualified a role. However there are a large number of voters who believe this new party is thinking along the right lines. Harry did not stand at the next election, so as to be able to devote all his time to running his group. He is also fortunate in having a very charming and talented wife, Bridget, with the ideal temperament for someone in her position.

Harry Oppenheimer is, of course, very wealthy by any standards and there are few causes that he is not prepared to support. Although he owns a number of houses and possesses a magnificent collection of paintings and other works of art, the Oppenheimers are really very simple people and have the common touch. Brenthurst, just outside Johannesburg, is their home, situated in a beautiful garden of some forty acres, and they entertain a great deal, as everyone who visits the country wants to meet them. I dined there a lot and enjoyed the delicious food.

Besides Brenthurst, they have several other houses. At Kimberley, where they have a stud, they have built a delightful house possessing every comfort, and it is a rare treat to stay there and be shown their magnificent collection of stallions and mares, foals and yearlings. They have taken up racing in a really big way and have been most successful, winning virtually all the important races in South Africa. I think they have twice won the Durban July Handicap, which was the most lucrative race in the country; and as my present group sponsors this event it's good to know that we have been instrumental in keeping the wolf from their door! Harry has been very clever in selecting his stallions from overseas, and he was one of the first to realize the need to import really good mares.

I first started running horses myself in 1948. Several of us encouraged Fred Rickaby, one of the famous Newmarket racing family, to come out and train for us, and this he did. He has been most successful and still trains in Natal. The very first horse I bought was a yearling called Country Fair. He only cost 500 guineas, and he won me something like fourteen races. He was, however, one of those 'in and outers'. On his day he could beat the best of them, but if he didn't feel like it no jockey could make him go. I had some awkward moments, and as I had become chairman of the Jockey Club in 1952 I had to be careful.

I remember a day in Durban which caused me considerable embarrassment. A week earlier Country Fair had run, and had been quite fancied. But it was not his day and he had failed miserably, much to my disappointment. On this particular day he was a 10–1 chance and we were far from hopeful. I was standing beside Fred Rickaby when the race started, and it soon became clear that Country Fair was not going to put it in. Five furlongs out he was tailed off and we could see through our glasses that he was not interested in spite of the efforts of the champion jockey who was riding him. Then suddenly Fred gripped my arm and shouted, 'Look, General, he's going to give it a go.' And sure enough the horse began gaining ground at an incredible rate; and in the end he won by a neck. I was, of course delighted as it was a big race—the Lonsdale Stirrup Cup. There was a fine trophy which was to be presented to the winning owner by the Mayor of Durban. I turned up at the unsaddling enclosure to receive it. When the great moment arrived the Mayor stepped forward to make his little speech. He had just started saying how pleased he was when boos and shouting split the air and I turned very red. However the trophy was handed over and I then had to go and explain the improved running of my horse to the Stewards. No action was taken because Country Fair's character was well known, but it gave me a bit of a jolt and wasn't very complimentary to the chairman of the Jockey Club!

Not long afterwards he again did the same sort of thing, but the other way round. He had won a good race by a distance and a few days later was a hot favourite for another race, carrying no penalty. All the newspapers had banner headlines suggesting that the race was at Country Fair's mercy, but he finished fourth. Soon after that I decided that he must go and I found a good home for this faithful but inconsistent old horse. I only wish horses could speak, as I would dearly have loved to have known why he behaved as he did.

I introduced a number of changes during my time. We started holding Jockey Club meetings at each of the main centres in order to give local members an opportunity of attending. The camera patrol was introduced, which proved a great success. This was some time before it was adopted in England. The Jockey Club secretary was a very able man named Dr Pfaff, and he pioneered this development. We also attacked the dope problem with great severity. But I could not persuade race clubs to introduce starting-pens. During my travels I had become convinced that these must come, but I met great opposition. Whenever I raised the issue at meetings or dinners, there were shouts of 'Never, never'. But today we use the pens in South Africa, the change having taken place after my time.

To finish this chapter about my life in South Africa, I must mention the Kruger National Park or Game Reserve. Although when a young soldier I lived amongst game for five years, I still get endless enjoyment visiting the park. It is so vast that you feel free and away from your normal way of life. In fact it is a real tonic. During these South African years I also enjoyed a delightful safari in Kenya with some old army friends of mine and their families, and had a really charming experience with a lioness: Sally, a legendary animal who lived in the bush east of the Mara river.

I am now a proud member of the World Wild Life Foundation and I feel really ashamed at the amount of game I shot in my younger days when serving with the King's African Rifles in Central Africa. Now I shoot with nothing more threatening than a camera!

Chapter Eight

Monty's Memoirs

I was kept very busy once I had joined the Tube Investments Group. We soon started expanding in South Africa, but I managed to visit Europe each year, partly for business reasons, partly to take some leave and see old friends. I even began to invest money for Montgomery in South African concerns—and our letters of 1948/9 are full of 'Glassworks at 8/9d' and 'Bolts and Rivets at 6/4d'.

There is no doubt that Monty was upset when General Eisenhower—just retiring as head of the US Army—published his wartime memoirs, *Crusade in Europe*, in 1948.

Why do it just now? [he asked me in a letter that December] Opening up controversial issues and giving his views on the character of his subordinates . . . We know he employed a ghost writer [a Press man], as he came over to London and saw some of my staff about certain points.

If you write about it, [he cautioned me in his usual way] I hope you will bring out clearly the points that :
1. He should not have opened up on issues that are very controversial.
2. He should not have analysed the characters of other war leaders.
3. Having done so, he has only himself to blame for the hoo-haa that is going on.

In a postscript, Monty added,

I think the real point is that we all love Ike and we all realise his immense contribution to winning the war. And we have all said so. And no British war leader has ever publicly criticised

him or anything he did. Everyone has paid tribute to him . . .
All the war leaders on our side of the Atlantic have remained
silent, though there is much we could say.

Ike's book conveys the impression that America won the
war; all British ideas were 'shot down' by Marshall and Ike.

Why has he done this? It is not good taste ! !

Three days later he wrote to me again,

Winston told me privately that he considers that Ike's book,
plus the Summersby book, have finished Ike as far as the
Presidency is concerned.

Events were to prove both Montgomery and Churchill quite
wrong—and Ike became not only the first Supreme Commander
of Allied Powers in Europe but subsequently, in 1952, one of the
best-loved presidents of America of all time.

In this respect Montgomery was a curious character; and he
never really forgave Eisenhower for his book, though he reserved
his own *coup de grâce* for another ten years. I suppose all sorts of
pressures combined on Monty at that time. At one level he was
undoubtedly altruistic: having won the war he wanted the
Western nations to 'win the peace', and hated to see dissension
between Britain and the USA. But was Ike's book really such a
threat to Anglo-American solidarity? Today *Crusade in Europe*
seems an unreadable and largely unread account of the Second
World War, with far too little controversial content in its 500
rather tedious pages!

No, it seems to me more likely, more in character, that Monty
was personally affected by Ike's references to him in the book;
tinged perhaps by a certain jealousy that Ike's military policy of
conquering Nazi Germany by muddled superiority should have
proved so successful in the end. Moreover Monty felt a certain
monopoly in controversy—and was undoubtedly caught off
balance by Eisenhower's public display of the art. It is true,
Monty's own two accounts (*Alamein to the Sangro*, and *Normandy to the Baltic*) were largely non-controversial: but they
began life as military education manuals and were ghosted by
David Belchem. The truth is that Monty always had difficulty in

seeing life through any but his own clear blue-grey eyes! Just as he never really appreciated Eisenhower's gift for combining political and military considerations, so too he failed to understand why Eisenhower should wish to put in print his entirely ingenuous convictions about the war and its chief protagonists in 1948.

I duly wrote a review of Ike's book for the London *Graphic*, pointing to Ike's perhaps less-than-fair account of Montgomery. Ike himself was quick to write to me, rebutting my reservations in a three-page letter. 'I went to great pains to show what I considered Monty's outstanding qualifications as a soldier to be,' he assured me. 'I know that you personally realize that inter-command relationships with some individuals were somewhat more difficult to maintain on an easy, comradely basis than were others . . . To attempt to conceal it would have elicited from many experienced soldiers the charge that the book was completely biased,' he pointed out—in my view quite rightly. It was inevitable that the war leaders would each one day pen their stories. I had myself done so the year before— and had been asked by Monty, as we have seen, to desist in future!

Once more—as in the war—I found myself trying to keep the peace between Eisenhower and Montgomery : not always an easy task. They were in almost every respect opposites; yet each in his own way a genius. Though Montgomery was fond of Ike, he never really took him seriously as a military professional— an attitude that pained Eisenhower deeply. For it was Eisenhower's peculiar, if not unique, talent to govern; to see and be seen to take the larger view. He made Monty his ground forces commander for the Normandy assault because it was logical to have one commander in such a co-ordinated tightly-knit operation; but he never intended Monty to retain the title afterwards— and took exception to a remark in my *Graphic* article that 'the best answer would have been to appoint a land force commander from the start'.

With regard to this view, [he wrote] I carefully pointed out in the book that such a plan would have conformed to British practice, but I still believed it to be absolutely wrong in any command so large as to include three Army Groups. In my

78

view each of these Army Group Commanders was a ground 'Commander in Chief' for a particular broad avenue of operation. To have inserted between these great field commanders and the Supreme Commander another echelon of command would have been, I feel, completely futile.

Contrasting with this larger view was Montgomery's own unashamedly military perception : the conviction that there ought not to have been three distinct army groups in the first place; and that you don't win victories by compromising but by relentless and informed leadership in the field.

In fact it was not very long before Montgomery and Eisenhower were back serving in the same team—this time at Supreme Headquarters Allied Powers in Europe in Paris, 1951 : an organization which both Montgomery and Eisenhower really created. For Montgomery, who had initially suffered from the obstructionism and jealousies of the French as chairman of the Western Union Forces, the arrival of Eisenhower at SHAPE— albeit as his boss—was very welcome. I offered my own services if times should become critical; and I am told my name went before the American Senate as Eisenhower's possible Chief of Staff. Montgomery too promised to rope me in 'quick enough if there is going to be any dirty work'—but his own view was that Russia had enough to contend with in Korea and the East to keep her occupied until at least 1952. 'In my view you should stay where you are and build up financial strength for your family,' he advised me.

I don't think he really enjoyed his job at SHAPE, for he could never get the politicians to agree priorities or decide what they would be prepared to do in certain eventualities. By September 1952 he was writing to me that he was 'ready to pack up from NATO next year after the Coronation. I shall have been 5 years in it then, i.e. since Oct. 1948, when I started the Western Union Military Organisation. By September 1953 I will be glad to pull out.' In fact he even promised to become a director of my company, Tube Investments, in 1954, after his retirement! However he had spent too long trying to make NATO a professional reality to chuck in his hand; and it was the very emergency behind the scenes that made him stay on.

Things are bad and NATO is moving to a crisis [he wrote to me in August 1953]. Rearmament has reached its financial peak and there will now be a decline; Marshall Aid will now cease. There is no agreed political aim, or strategic aim, on a global scale. We are drifting towards chaos . . . Winston is ill and can never be the same.

I stayed in the White House for a week with Ike, and we discussed every problem at length. He is very well. We have got rid of Ridgway; . . . He refused to take advice.

The reader can no doubt imagine whose!

That year also saw the publication of my second book. It was called *African Assignment* and dealt with my early days in Africa when serving with the King's African Rifles. It was not a subject which had a particularly wide appeal and therefore did not sell very well.

After many years the doctors eventually found out what had been giving me so much trouble during the war years and afterwards. I had nurtured a large gall-stone. Repeated X-rays had never shown it up. Apparently it had always been obscured by a rib. Within two days I had the operation and the offending stone was removed. I couldn't help thinking what a lot of trouble I would have been saved if that rib hadn't played such an unkindly trick. When I had completely recovered, Ted Crane, the ex-cycle king, asked me to join him in his yacht for a two-week cruise in the Mediterranean. Ivan Stedeford was one of the guests and we spent a very happy time visiting Corsica, Sardinia, Capri and Italy.

It was towards the end of 1955, because of certain domestic problems, that I began to think seriously about the possibility of returning to work in England. I therefore wrote to Stedeford and told him that, if he wanted it that way, I might be prepared to come back and take up the position of deputy chairman. In his reply he wisely did not commit himself and suggested that I should be attached to the group for three or four months so as to get to know everyone and then see how I felt about things; but he also implied that it would be necessary to convince some of the more senior TI executives that I was the right man for the job. I saw the wisdom of his proposals and it was arranged that I should report for duty in April 1956.

Soon after my arrival the chairman suggested I should make a thorough investigation of the group and produce a report for him. This meant a lot of travelling, but I enjoyed visiting the many companies and talking to the men on the spot about their problems. I learned a great deal in the process. TI was a vast empire with its steel plants, tube-making factories, and with other divisions that consisted of heavy engineering, electrical equipment of all sorts, bicycles, aluminium and other products. Besides this I interviewed several chairmen of some of the largest British concerns, e.g. ICI, Stewart & Lloyds, Unilever, Dunlop etc. And of course I discussed various matters with the directors who sat on the main TI board. It was a wonderful self-education and after I'd collected sufficient information I set about looking at the way TI was run, taking into account the views expressed by those within our group as well as those gathered from outside. The end result was a pretty comprehensive report in which I analysed our strengths and weaknesses and put forward a number of recommendations. It was quite clear to me that TI's rapid growth had not been sufficiently appreciated and that some reorganization was desirable. In particular I felt Stedeford himself carried a tremendous load being both chairman and managing director. I won't go into details, but I have a copy of my report before me and it is interesting to see that most of my recommendations have since been introduced; the majority however after Lord Plowden took over TI as chairman.

Having had my report typed by a confidential typist, the time arrived to present it to Stedeford. I went round to his flat about 6 p.m. one evening, gave him the report and said, 'I'll leave you to read it, for it will take you quite a time. When you've finished come round to White's Club and we'll have dinner. I'll expect you about 8 o'clock.'

Just before 8 I was standing by the bar when I spotted Ivan being led towards me by the club porter. The moment I saw him it was clear that he wasn't very enthusiastic about my report. I greeted him and asked him what he would like to drink. Having ordered what he wanted, Wheeler passed it over and we drank slowly and silently. Eventually Stedeford said, 'I don't think I agree with much of your report.' I made some indefinite reply, and finishing our drinks we walked upstairs to enjoy the excellent food that White's always provides. I purposely kept off the subject of the report and we talked of other things.

After dinner we went back to his flat and then in a very short time my chairman proceeded to pull my report to pieces. I listened and made only a few comments. After he had finished I decided that even if he still wanted me to become deputy chairman, it would never work, and so I told him that I had completed my task and thought the best thing for me to do would be to go back to South Africa. This was agreed to, and in retrospect I'm very glad it worked out that way.

The next two years were reasonably uneventful businesswise. I spent most of my time in South Africa, other than my usual few weeks' visit to Europe.

I did however continue to correspond with my old wartime bosses—and became embroiled in both the Suez affair and, later, the publication of Monty's controversial *Memoirs*.

Although I was living in South Africa and leading the life of a businessman, I had always kept up my interest in army and defence matters, giving many speeches and writing many articles. Looking through my scrapbooks I'm sure I spoke and wrote too much! But I find that my predictions of how the world would develop from the military point of view were surprisingly accurate. During the Korean War the *Rand Daily Mail* had commissioned me to write a daily article on the progress of operations. This was really quite a task, situated as I was many thousands of miles away from the theatre of war, but I found it rather fun. I also wrote about the Suez crisis in 1956. I was very critical from the start as I was certain the plan would fail and I could never understand how the British Chiefs of Staff had ever given their blessing to the conditions that were laid down by the politicians. Because of the eight-day time-lag between the initial bombing attacks on Egypt and the landing of the troops, it looked certain to me that America, the United Nations and Russia would have time to react unfavourably and doom the operation to failure. And in the end I was proved right.

One evening I was dining at White's Club in London with Anthony Head, who was then Minister of Defence, a few days before the attack was due to start. He hinted what was about to take place and even asked for my advice—we had known each other during the war and had kept in close touch ever since. I was horrified when I heard of the outline plan and I remember late at night taking a piece of notepaper and writing out about half a dozen questions which I suggested he should put to the Chiefs of Staff. I did not, for instance, agree with the view that the Egyptians would be capable of putting up much of a fight; and therefore I felt there was no need to have this unfortunate delay between the bombing attacks on their air force and the landing of the army. I was convinced risks could be taken. But Eden was determined on this plan and I believe had laid down that casualties must be extremely few. What a way to fight a war! But I had had experience of Eden in the disastrous British expedition to Greece in 1941, and was not altogether surprised. However, to undertake this campaign without passing on any information whatever to Britain's good friend Eisenhower, who was then President of the United States, was a cardinal error. I know there were risks as to possible American reaction, but keeping him in ignorance courted disaster.

At the time Eisenhower was in no doubt that his allies had acted wrongly—but wrote to me from the White House that he had

never for one moment wavered in my feeling of friendship for our traditional allies or in my search for ways and means to help them out of the difficulties that, in my opinion, they brought upon themselves by their hasty and ill-considered action.

The measures we have already taken and which are contemplated are going to cost us a huge sum during the coming two years; I think it will gradually be understood in Western Europe that we have been a *true* friend throughout this entire affair. I do not conceive it to be the function of a friend to encourage action that he believes in his heart to be unwise and even inexpedient . . . Let us pray that this thing will work out as well as we can possibly expect.

In later years he was prepared to admit that America might have been wrong over Suez, which rapidly became the kernel of the Middle East problem; but he never ceased to ascribe the blame to Eden for 'the deplorable way he handled the whole affair'.

Monty meanwhile had remained at SHAPE, but had since 1955 been working on his *Memoirs*. By February 1956 he had finished all the early chapters up to June 1944. 'It has been pronounced "very good" by Bill Williams, P. J. Grigg and Arthur Bryant,' he wrote to me full of self-confidence, '—which ought to be good enough!' And by January 1957 he had finished the book. However, he had decided not to retire from NATO until June 1958, when he would have served fifty years in the Army; so until then the large case of dynamite remained unopened. Monty however had no illusions about the eventual eruption it would cause. 'You can take it that it will create quite a stir in Whitehall, and it may be that I will find it convenient to be out of England on the day it is published!!' he wrote.

In the spring of 1958 he wrote again, promising the book would 'create an immense sensation'—but not offering to show the manuscript to me. In fact so sure was he that Eisenhower would not be hurt that he had quite happily arranged to fly to Washington 'to stay with Ike' in May—only months before publication began!

Of course the *Memoirs did* cause a stir, and the writs—or the threat of them—were soon flying. Monty was like a small boy; he had waited thirteen years since the war to get certain matters off his chest, and the excitement of the *Memoirs* being published no doubt distracted him from the whole question of what one does in retirement.

Field-Marshal Auchinleck was the first to take offence, for Monty's version of his takeover in the desert in August 1942 was, to say the least, uncharitable. In the end Monty had to make a broadcast accepting that the Auk had stabilized the situation at Alamein before being removed from command; and a disclaimer was incorporated by Collins in subsequent editions of the *Memoirs* and in the Press. But as regards a more personal reconciliation, Monty was adamant.

I am entirely opposed to your entering what people are pleased to call the Monty/Auk contest [he wrote to me just before Christmas 1958]. It has now died down and the Press are on to other things. The notice in the *Sunday Times* in December has settled it so far as the Press are concerned. A letter like the one you suggest would cause the whole affair to flare up again and my telephone will then ring all day with the Press asking for my reactions. *Least said, soonest mended.* For God's sake leave it alone.

And don't ask me to the dinner party [with Auchinleck] you suggest in your last para. I would decline. The Press would be on to it at once.

Your suggested letter will not 'kill the whole business' as you say. It will cause the whole thing to flare up again. I would then have to say that I adhere to what I have written—which I do, and don't want to have to say.

So pipe down—please.

I note you say the Auk admires *me*. But I don't admire him —and never have from the day I first served under him in the Southern Command after Dunkirk. That experience was enough for me.

This was certainly a far cry from the quiet dignity of Auchinleck himself—who, as he wrote to me, had nothing but admiration for Monty's achievements and qualities, but was determined to remove the slur that Monty had 'cast on many brave and able soldiers who served under me . . . It is a pity that he lets his pen and his tongue run away with him, as he injures and angers many worthy people who did their best in difficult times. However, there it is.'

Eisenhower was equally, if not more, deeply offended; but once again Monty would neither go back on what he had said nor even attempt a personal reconciliation. From that moment Eisenhower—who declined to read the actual book—refused to have anything more to do with Monty; and to the time of his death he never wrote again to his erstwhile friend and colleague. Monty simply failed to see why, when he had said so many nice things about Eisenhower in the *Memoirs*, Ike should take exception to the nasty things he'd said. Yet for Eisenhower the assertion that as Supreme Commander he had prolonged the war by six months was an insult which, as both human being and President still of the United States, he deeply resented. 'It doesn't help if he accuses me of prolonging the war an extra six months, and therefore being responsible for the slaughter of unnecessary lives, and then adds that "I'm a great friend of his and he is a wonderful chap," ' he once said to me. When I mooted a possible visit by

Monty to the White House in the summer of 1959 to make up their differences, Eisenhower was quite categorical.

It would likely be bad judgement, at this particular time, for Monty to make any attempt to visit me [he wrote].

I assure you that my feeling is merely one of disappointment, not of rancor. Even Winston, when he was here, remarked that obviously I felt little personal resentment towards Monty's publicity endeavors because he (Winston) had noted that, in our living quarters on the second floor at the White House, Monty's picture occupied the same place as in former years.

My feelings about any visit apply also to any explanatory statement Monty might conceivably make about the affair. He obviously cannot retreat from a public position he has already made clear; consequently there would be no hope of such a statement making for better 'allied' feeling. Likewise, I think any correspondence between us could not be very helpful because of the reason that Monty, both by publication and broadcasts, has made the whole matter a public affair, not a private one.

All this is, of course, negative. But I feel that if the matter is to be healed in any way, that *time* will have to be relied on as the healer.

Time, unfortunately, never healed the breach. Though the American Ambassador brought both men together at a reunion banquet in London later that year, the ice had not melted; nor did it ever. Ike had perhaps been too patient, too understanding, for too long; and the longer Monty stored up such a pronouncement, the more cruel it appeared to him.

Monty was perhaps too excited by his literary success to care— or if he did, he was not one to show it. He joined our company, Tube Investments, as a consultant, and in November 1959 visited South Africa—where he formed a very positive opinion of the state and its efforts at a balanced solution to the racial problem. Certainly he didn't lack the courage to say what most Western politicians and leaders felt but didn't dare repeat aloud: that the 'white' solution in South Africa was incalculably more civilized

86

than the examples provided by the emerging black African states—both for whites and for blacks; and in the years from 1962 he began to voyage every January to Cape Town for health and relaxation.

Chapter Nine

The Chair of British Aluminium

Meanwhile, towards the end of 1958, when in London, Stedeford told me of his plans for making a takeover bid for British Aluminium. This company fabricated the metal in the United Kingdom, operated two small smelters in Scotland, and had just opened a big smelter in Canada, at a place called Bai Comeau on the north shore of the St. Lawrence estuary some 300 miles east of Quebec. They also had a plant in Scotland for producing alumina, the substance from which the metal is smelted. They owned bauxite deposits in various countries and had a joint company with Consolidated Zinc in Australia, called Comalco. This company owned substantial bauxite deposits in the Northern Territories and in Queensland. They were also hoping to buy the government-owned smelter at Bell Bay in Tasmania.

Tube Investments had their own aluminium division which was shared with Reynolds Metals of the USA on a 51%–49% basis. TI Aluminium owned several factories for fabricating the metal, but had to import most of the metal from overseas.

When TI and Reynolds Metals became interested in British Aluminium, a takeover bid had already been made by Alcosa, the American company, and at a certain stage the British Aluminium board had recommended shareholders to accept the offer. But then we stepped in and an historic battle took place which really shook the City. The British Aluminium board were keen that the Alcosa deal should go through and did not approve of our intervention. I believe Stedeford was sent for by the Governor of the Bank of England and also by the Chancellor, to advise caution as to how he proceeded. But in spite of these exhortations the battle went on and the price offered for the shares rose, until TI won the day. In letters to me at the end of 1958, Stedeford expressed his concern that the BA

88

board had by their attitude helped to produce such a distressing situation. A final effort to defeat us took the form of a counter-bid made by a consortium organized by Lazards. But even this failed. I think the final offer cost TI and Reynolds Metals over £35,000,000.

It was some time in January 1959 that Stedeford rang me up in Johannesburg one evening and reported that TI/Reynolds had obtained the required percentage of acceptances, and therefore the battle had been won. I congratulated him and wished the new company all success. I think it was the next night that he rang again. He started by explaining that a lot of wounds had been inflicted during the takeover battle and a number of noses had been put out of joint. He went on to say there was a big job to be done to heal these wounds and to convince the various British Aluminium interests around the world that TI were not such scoundrels as some people might think they were. He said he thought he knew the right man to carry out this task. I thought for a moment and came to the conclusion that he had a certain mutual friend in mind. So I mentioned his name and said I would try to persuade him to take it on. He quickly interrupted me by saying that he had been referring to me.

My initial reaction was that this was the last thing I wanted to do. I had made my home in South Africa for a number of years, all my belongings and interests were here, and in any case the last time I had offered to serve with TI in England had ended up in failure. He asked me to think it over, because he really wanted some help, and said he would ring me again in a day or two. He rang again in two days' time and after a long talk I agreed to go over for three to four months at the most, and this seemed to satisfy my Chief. I handed things over to Jack Catling, my deputy, knowing that he would have a big job in front of him as the Raleigh/TI agreement in South Africa was on the point of being signed; and I arrived back in London on a cold and miserable January day, putting up at the Army & Navy Club.

The next day I received a thorough briefing about our new acquisition, British Aluminium. I heard the details of the emotional battle that had taken place, and it soon became obvious that there must be many wounds, and deep ones too. It was agreed that the chairman, Air Chief Marshal Lord Portal, and the managing director, would depart with generous golden handshakes, but the remaining executive directors would be asked to carry on. Then I was told about the company's overseas interests in France, Canada, Australia, Guinea, etc., and I could see that these had to be handled with considerable care. It reminded me of the war years when I had spent a lot of my time smoothing over difficulties that had arisen between Montgomery and Eisenhower and others. 'You had better go and meet the top executives in BA,' I was told, and in reply to my question as to whether anyone from TI had yet visited their head office, the answer was 'No one.' So we sent a message to British Aluminium's company secretary to say that I proposed to call the following morning.

BA's head office was in Norfolk House in St James's Square, the very place where SHAEF had had their headquarters for a time before D-Day. It was where the preliminary planning had taken place and after my return to 21st Army Group, I had spent a lot of time there attending conferences with Eisenhower and other service chiefs. So it was an entirely suitable place to conduct a campaign in the industrial world! I got out of my car, glanced at the plaque fixed to the wall which consisted of the SHAEF badge, with an inscription below to commemorate the fact that Eisenhower's headquarters had been located there, nodded at the commissionaire who was sitting at his desk, and stepped into a lift which was on the point of going up. Having just made it I glanced up to see who were my travelling companions. To my surprise and I may add also to my embarrassment, there was the outgoing chairman of BA, Lord Portal. I hadn't met him since the war and, other than giving him a polite smile, I didn't open my mouth.

I gradually got to know the executive directors who by and large were good men, but the recent happenings had produced an effect on morale. I made it my business to get to know these people and what was more important, to learn something about the company, its organization, and its various operations. Before long I was getting excellent co-operation and every night I took back to my club a mass of papers, reports and studies. I spent a miserable two weeks or more sitting in my bedroom each evening, reading away and making pages of notes. The weather was horrible, cold and foggy, and I pined for my lovely house and garden in Johannesburg in the summer-time. I asked myself why

I had been so foolish as to agree to leave South Africa. As the days wore on I began to see daylight and soon Stedeford was pressing me to visit Australia as he considered the situation there was probably the most delicate.

I think I managed to convince the BA executives that TI and Reynolds were reasonable people and that they had little to fear from the new control. We were out to help them rather than hinder them. I found a certain amount of concern about the Reynolds Metals set-up, which I presumed emanated from battling against them in the world markets. A high priority task was to soothe some of the individuals and firms in the city who had had their fingers burnt during the takeover battle. I first went to see Lazards, the merchant bankers, who had done their best to defeat TI. I knew Tommy Brand (later Lord Hampden) very well and had a long session with him explaining our point of view. In the end I found him very reasonable. I also saw Oliver Poole (later Lord Poole) who served under me in the Eighth Army and 21st Army Group. He looked after the Cowdray fortunes which in fact controlled Lazards. We talked the same language and I left feeling we had no problems there. I also saw stockbrokers and others and at the end felt that the wounds were healing very nicely.

Before I left for Australia Stedeford asked me to join him for a couple of days at an hotel in Bournemouth, so that we could have a quiet talk and perhaps, weather permitting, a game of golf. For two evenings we sat up talking about British Aluminium, but also about my position. He wanted me to commit myself to remaining in England but I found it extremely difficult to tie him down in what capacity I would be required to function. I wanted some specific assurances on my position, as I was against being kept on standby until something out of the ordinary cropped up. In the end it was mutually agreed that we'd more or less play it by ear.

Some time in February I flew to Australia. It was extremely hot in Sydney when I arrived, but cooler in Melbourne, which was my destination. There I met my future colleagues on the Comalco Board. Bill Robinson, the son of a great Australian industrialist, was the chairman and was also chairman of that powerful group, Consolidated Zinc. There was Morry Mawby, who later took over from Bill Robinson; Don Hibbert, a great man to have on your side; and Walter Rice who was a Reynolds Metals man and later became United States Ambassador in Canberra. There was a refreshing atmosphere to be found at these meetings: great optimism and a desire to push ahead and develop our bauxite deposits; erect an alumina plant and purchase from the Government the Bell Bay smelter. All this would need a great deal of finance and the two new partners were beginning to hesitate about the ultimate cost. Walter Rice was very bullish about the future demand for the metal, but some of us could not go with him all the way. To me it was quite an experience to see how our Australian colleagues were prepared to take risks, as they had tremendous faith in the future of their country.

During my attachment to BA I visited Australia two or three times and during one of my trips a delegation of the board flew over to Canberra to attend a Cabinet committee formed to discuss with us the purchase of the Bell Bay smelter. Don Hibbert had done his homework very well and we had firm proposals to put to the Government. The construction of this smelter had been a wartime measure and we knew that it was government policy to sell out to private enterprise.

The Prime Minister himself, Bob Menzies, was chairman of the Cabinet committee appointed to meet us. I remember being extremely impressed by the way this great statesman handled the meeting. He hardly had a note in front of him, but gave a most detailed and informative review of the whole problem. It was a real *tour de force* and it cleared the decks so that we could all get down to business. When our turn came we explained what we would be prepared to pay, and in what way, and over what period. This was not something that could be settled over a Cabinet table, as besides the financial aspects, politics came into it. Eventually the meeting broke up after considerable discussion and we were left to await developments.

After the meeting Bob Menzies asked me into his office for a drink, which by then I really needed. 'Your old Chief is coming out here as you know,' he said, and then went on to tell me how Monty had been pressurizing him by degrees in order to get what he wanted. First it was for the appointment of an ADC to look after him during his visit. Then he asked the Government to make all arrangements for his internal flights and accommodation, and finally he asked for an aircraft to be placed at his disposal for the whole period he would be in the country. Menzies concluded: 'Knowing old Monty usually got what he wanted in the end, I'm laying it all on!'

When in Australia I received word that I had been appointed to the top Tube Investments board. But this news I have to admit did not excite me very much since I had already joined the board of British Aluminium.

On my return to London I set about a programme of visiting the various British Aluminium plants and establishments. I felt rather like a general taking over a new command and visiting his formations and units. I did my best to put over a reasonable TI image and I think succeeded. I was particularly fascinated by our two small smelters located in Scotland—one at Fort William and another a few miles away at Kinlochleven. Very cheap power is essential for operating an aluminium smelter and so BA had constructed two small hydro-electric plants to serve the smelters. The country in that part of Scotland is glorious, and I enjoyed these visits greatly.

I forget exactly when I met my Reynolds' colleague, Louis Reynolds, who had been chosen to look after their BA interests, but it was fairly early in 1959. I had better describe two of the Reynolds family. Richard was the head of Reynolds Metals and Louis was the chairman or president of Reynolds International. They were both very colourful characters. They lived in Richmond, Virginia, and were of good old Southern stock. Richard was extremely able, with a great zest for life. Besides working hard at his business he hunted, shot and raced horses. His wife Virginia was as charming as she was good-looking. Louis was a ball of fire. Ideas poured out of his head at the rate of knots. It was often quite bewildering and this sometimes made co-operation a little difficult. But every now and then he produced a brainwave. He came flitting in and out of England with bewildering frequency, rarely staying long enough to get down to brass tacks. But he was very stimulating and we used to play golf and gamble at backgammon and other games. The two brothers were very short in height and sturdy in build. I got to know them both very well and liked them quite a lot.

Once they asked me over to Virginia to see the Kentucky Derby. My daughter Marylou was also invited. We all took off from Richmond in various company aircraft for Louisville. In our plane, a DC6, we had a great time, as an excellent lunch was provided and we gambled at various games of chance throughout the journey. It was their custom each year to rent two or three villas for their guests to stay in, so every comfort was provided. There was of course an exhausting round of social events, and finally the great day arrived. If you haven't attended this famous race-meeting, it is well worth the effort. Every place in every stand appeared to be full, and I noticed segregation was pretty well enforced. It was a hot day and during the afternoon waiters came round carrying trays of mint juleps, which were consumed by the racegoers at an astonishing tempo. It was not surprising therefore that when the great moment arrived, just before the race was due to start, and the massed bands played 'My Old Kentucky Home', many people burst into tears. I must admit I felt considerable emotion myself because as everyone sang this haunting melody, one's thoughts went back to the gracious days enjoyed in the South before the Civil War.

During one of our visits the Quebec Premier, Maurice du Plessis, was invited to spend a night and dine with us. I was quite nauseated by the way our American friends treated him. It was flattery on the grand scale, but afterwards I was assured that this was necessary because in those days one couldn't obtain one's power or other requirements without ingratiating oneself with the Premier and making considerable contributions to party funds, which the Premier made use of for his political ends. I'm glad to say things have changed a lot since then. I met the present Premier of Canada, Pierre Trudeau, a few years ago and was most impressed with his stature and the sensible views he held. He was a young man in his thirties.

BA had managed over the years to acquire certain 'perks' or fringe benefits. Because of their hydro-electric power schemes in Scotland they owned large tracts of land. There were two grouse moors and some excellent stalking available. Unfortunately the grouse had more or less disappeared and although some good shooting was to be had before the war, when I became a director there was little to be had. The stalking on the other hand is still excellent and, for a reasonable fee, it is available for BA personnel.

Another asset was a yacht. It was built entirely of aluminium and because of this the tax authorities had allowed it as a legitimate expense. The idea behind it was to encourage the use

94

of the metal for large as well as small yachts. Her name was *Morag Mohr* and she had an excellent crew of two, who came from Scotland.

Because of my efforts with BA I asked for its use for the long August bank holiday weekend, and this was arranged. I took along my daughter, my brother Buster who was a great yachtsman, and his wife and daughter. The yacht was lying in Southampton water and we sailed from there about lunch-time for Le Havre, which we reached in the early hours of the morning. After some difficulty we found a harbour official who led us to the yacht basin where we tied up and got some well earned sleep. After shopping the next morning, we started our journey under power along the canals which run more or less parallel with the Seine. By 6 p.m. we had reached the beautiful Tankeaurville Suspension bridge, and after a long wait in the final lock entered the Seine proper.

We aimed at reaching a place called Caudebec which is a few miles below Rouen. As it was getting dark, we decided to drop anchor and have a really good dinner ashore. On our arrival in the gloaming, the staff of a restaurant situated close to the river bank lined up and made welcoming signs. The chef, wearing his white hat, was extremely fat and my brother advised me to have our dinner here. 'You can't go wrong with a fat chef,' he said. And how right he was! We had a really superb dinner and I shall never forget a dish of *écrevisses* which he produced. The next day we started our return journey down the Seine and only just reached Honfleur in time, as the tide was ebbing. We got stuck in the mud at the harbour entrance, but managed to get off again before it was too late. It was a Sunday evening and only by my brother jumping ashore and ferreting out one of the harbour staff were we able to get the lock gates, which sealed off the yacht basin, opened in time. We were thankful for this because otherwise we would have spent the night on our side in the outer harbour. We tied up alongside the quay and cooked an excellent dinner.

It was a joy to wake up the next morning to see this charming little harbour in sunlight. Surrounded by old houses with different coloured shutters, the scene was a very gay one and I felt like playing truant and hi-jacking this delightful yacht and sailing her away to the Med. However realism soon returned. There was shopping to be done, and we were due to leave the yacht basin at about 10 a.m. when the tide had risen sufficiently.

After a few months I moved from my London Club to a delightful little house in Hays Mews. It belonged to some great friends of mine, Harry and Ghislaine Cubitt. As my house backed on theirs in Charles Street, we saw a great deal of each other, spending weekends at various houses, playing golf, racing and shooting together. Later Harry became Lord Ashcombe and we are still close friends.

After Lord Plowden took over TI I found my work with BA had more or less come to an end and I began to make noises about returning to South Africa once again. Stedeford pressed me to stay on—but again with no specific appointment in mind. Then one day he said, 'Freddie, do you think you could persuade George Wilson to sell out Raleigh Industries to TI?' As this company had had an excellent year, I expressed some doubt and suggested it might be easier to persuade George Wilson to make an offer for our cycle interests. Personally I did not take a very optimistic view as to the future of the bicycle industry in the UK. But Stedeford pointed out certain difficulties of doing a deal this way, and so I agreed to see what I could achieve.

I made contact with George Wilson again, which was a real pleasure. I stayed with him a couple of times and fished with him on the Wye. All the time I did my best to persuade him to sell out. At first he wouldn't hear of it and, as I expected, offered to buy us out. I explained we would not disturb the management and that he would remain chairman. As they had built a very large factory in Nottingham, it was obvious this would be used as the main production unit. Also he would have full powers to rational-ize production and close down any of TI's factories that became superfluous. After numerous discussions I eventually got things to the point where he and Stedeford should meet to agree on the price to be paid. I was present on this occasion and I could see what a hard decision this was for George to make. He had been highly successful in building up Raleigh and he hated having to sell out to another group. However in the end a price per share was agreed on and his shareholders did quite well out of it. I can't say the same for TI. The cycle market slumped, particularly the export market to the USA. Great difficulties were experienced with the trade unions because of the closing down of factories and

96

the question of redundancy payments. Strikes occurred and production difficulties were numerous. However now, I'm glad to say, the American market is booming.

After the deal I was involved in a small way in negotiations with the trade unions about the closing down of a TI cycle factory in Ashford, Kent. It had been a very successful little business and it was run by Fred Norman and his brother who had owned the company before it was bought by TI. The move was most unpopular with the management and the local authorities, but it had to be done. I felt very sorry for Fred Norman who was a friend of mine. I had never had to deal with trade union officials in England before, and so I looked forward to the experience. We had several meetings and I spoke to all the employees together, as well as with the shop stewards and the trade union officials. Together we worked out a plan for closing down the factory, redundancy payments etc. I found the officials co-operative and understanding. They wanted a fair deal for their members and I agreed that they should have one. In fact they told me that if only management tackled such matters with the unions the way I had, labour relations would be much better. But suddenly I was told to hand over the negotiations to someone else, and I have an uneasy suspicion that the final settlement was not as fair and generous as I had hoped. If this was so, it was a pity.

It was a sad blow when a year or two later George Wilson was killed in a car smash when returning home from a day's shooting. I lost a very dear friend.

Stedeford and I used to dine together each week in London for relaxation and to discuss any problems within TI that needed attention. Towards the end of 1960 I told him one evening that I considered it time that I should think about returning to South Africa. He said, 'Surely you don't mean that—you must be mad.' I explained once again that I had made my home there and most of my outside interests were in that country. I pointed out that I had joined TI when I was resident and domiciled in that country, and therefore there was no obligation on my part to return to the UK. He didn't appear to think I was serious, but I reminded him that I had no specific job and was only being used to tackle any unexpected problems as they occurred. This was not a very satisfactory position to be in at my age. I also was rather tired of living away from my own home and personal

D*   97

belongings. Having stated my intention, I let the matter rest there for the time being.

In November I had a phone call that changed my future industrial life. I was sitting in my little house in Hays Mews one evening when the telephone rang and Dr Anton Rupert, a prominent and successful South African industrialist, asked to speak to me. I knew him slightly and had followed his meteoric rise. He was a magnificent man, very human and open-minded in his views. He said he would like to see me about an urgent matter, so I suggested he should come round after dinner that very night. I had met this delightful and able South African a few times before, but did not know him very well. He arrived on time and I mixed him a drink and we sat down. Anton came straight to the point and said, 'Sir Francis, I would like you to join my group.' This was certainly a big surprise and I began thinking what my reply would be. But Rupert started to describe his group, how it had grown and how just recently he had acquired 50% of the voting shares of a tobacco firm called Carreras, which was based in London. The eldest Baron brother who controlled the company had sold out his holding. I asked a few questions and then told him I was very flattered at the suggestion but in view of my TI activities I thought it might be difficult to take on another sizeable job. Rupert assured me he would be quite happy if I only worked half-time for him. In the end I told him I would think about it, but much depended upon my future position with Tube Investments. We agreed to keep in touch. I was very intrigued by this offer, for the progress of the Rembrandt/Rothmans group had been a fantastic story of success.

Not long after this meeting I had to return to South Africa for a short visit in order to attend one or two annual general meetings, particularly the AGM of the South Africa Foundation, of which I was president, but more of this later.

The South Africa Foundation AGM was being held at the Carlton Hotel in Johannesburg and was an all-day affair. Anton Rupert was one of the many trustees attending, and during the afternoon session I received a note from him in which he invited me to come up to his suite for a cup of tea when the proceedings were over. I arrived about 4.30 p.m. and there he was surrounded by several of his young men examining cigarette packages and advertising material. This was a scene I came to know so well.

On this occasion he told his people to leave us alone. The door had hardly shut before Anton turned to me and said, 'Now, Sir Francis, have you made up your mind?' I replied that I could not be certain but would see Stedeford on my return, making it quite clear that I intended returning to South Africa and trying to get his agreement to my joining this world-wide tobacco group. He then said, 'I think we should discuss remuneration,' and went straight on to suggest a certain figure, which struck me as being generous in view of the fact that I would only be working on a half-time basis. After a few minutes' pleasant chat I left, and within two days I was back in England again.

Almost immediately after my return I rang up Ivan Stedeford and asked if I could come and stay with him at his country house in Warwickshire the coming Saturday night. He willingly agreed and I looked forward to meeting the family again whom I had, over the years, got to know very well. After lunch on the Sunday I asked Ivan if we could move to his study for a talk. I started by reiterating that my intention was to return to South Africa in the near future. We went over all the old arguments and once again Stedeford told me he thought I was being very foolish. He then proceeded to put on a bit of pressure which was, I thought, un-worthy of him. He said, 'You know TI's operations in South Africa are now running very smoothly, and in any case are comparatively small. Therefore I don't know whether we would be justified in paying you what we do today.' This nettled me as the satisfactory situation was in some measure due to my efforts and it was unusual for a top executive to have his remuneration reduced at my time of life.

But I played it another way. I said that I agreed to what he said about TI's affairs in South Africa, and I thought that it would only take up half of my time. Stedeford nodded his head. I went on to say that this being the case, then it was logical that I should receive half my previous salary. Stedeford showed his disagreement and said, 'Oh, now, Freddie, don't be silly, I didn't mean to go to that length.' However I stuck to my point and stressed that in view of what he had said this would be a fair solution, but as I was still young and active enough, I presumed he had no objection to my taking on another half-time job. At first he reacted unfavourably, saying that TI didn't permit their directors to work for other companies. I then had to remind him

99

that in my letter of appointment I had specifically suggested a clause which allowed me to take on other work provided it did not interfere with my TI duties. And as we both agreed that only half my time would be taken up with our affairs in South Africa, I considered I was permitted to use the other half of my time in other directions. He did not appear to remember what was contained in the letter of appointment, so I suggested he had a look at it when he arrived in London the next day.

On the Monday I called at his office and by then he had seen the letter and had to agree that I was right. Soon afterwards I called Rupert accepting his offer. As Ivan and I were very close friends after all these years, we didn't let this little contretemps upset our relationship, but it meant that I now had the green light to go ahead and accept Anton Rupert's offer. I had decided to return by boat in the following May with my daughter, who was then at a finishing school in Switzerland. For the remainder of my time with TI in London, I carried out various tasks, including a final visit to Bai Comeau in Canada to deal with a rather delicate personnel problem.

So drew to a close a few hectic years of my life as an industrialist. They had been exciting years but also rather disturbing years, though on the whole I wouldn't have missed them for all the tea in China.

Chapter Ten

The Rupert Empire—and Farewell to Monty

I must tell you something about my new group chairman, Dr Anton Rupert, and the history of the 'empire' which he started. It is quite a story. First the man. He was born in 1916 at Graaf-Reinet, a small town on the edge of the Karoo. He obtained a degree in applied chemistry at the University of Pretoria and studied law and commerce at the University of South Africa. He married his handsome and gifted wife Hubert in 1941. At this time he was a lecturer in chemistry, but soon his pent-up energy began to look for new outlets. He started building a small dry-cleaning business in Pretoria and not long afterwards sold out at a profit. He next turned his attention to the highly competitive tobacco industry, where the powerful British American Tobacco group had a virtual monopoly in South Africa. Equipment in this immediate post-war era was extremely hard to get. However, with no previous knowledge of the market, but with that boundless energy and drive that he has displayed throughout his industrial career, he managed to obtain two antiquated cigarette or tobacco processing machines in Canada after the war. It was only in 1948 that he had acquired the necessary raw materials and plant to start the manufacture of pipe tobacco etc. in earnest.

In the meantime he began a wine and spirit concern called Distillers Corporation (SA) Ltd., which today has grown into a large Group and is one of the world's largest distiller's of brandy.

To raise the initial capital, he went from one farmer to the other, selling them shares in his new company at five shillings each. Those original shares must be worth at least twenty-five times that value today. Having raised the small initial capital he required, and with his cigarette plant established in an old mill at Paarl in the Cape, the young Rupert was ready to accept the challenge. From this small beginning, the group today ranks in fourth or fifth place in the world's cigarette production, with fifty factories situated in twenty-three countries on five continents. No small achievement in twenty-five years.

In the late forties Rupert met a fascinating character called Paddy O'Neil-Dunne who was connected with a small British company called Rothmans of Pall Mall, and he reached an agreement to manufacture their cigarettes in South Africa in exchange for Rothmans' industrial know-how. Rupert's main objective at that time was to make 'every cigarette a masterpiece'. Being a chemist he was very conscious of the importance of research and in 1952 his company produced the world's first king-size filter cigarette. This was a tremendous money-spinner in most countries of the world. Then in 1953 he bought out Rothmans of London, and from that point never looked back. He attacked country by country, as well as the export markets of the world.

He was now manufacturing in South Africa and England, and the time had come to tackle the 'big boys' in their well established areas. Great courage and faith were necessary and he was picking his team of young and enthusiastic men to carry out his plans. Paddy O'Neil-Dunne was just the man to lead the task forces into foreign lands, which he did with great effect. He employed rather unorthodox methods and operated with a sort of happy abandon. But it paid dividends, as the opposition were, at this time, feeling a bit smug, if I may use the term, owing to the strong positions they had established.

The first target was Australia, where the new king-size filter cigarette swept the board and before long this aggressive little company had acquired over 50% of the total market. From Australia it was not a long hop to New Zealand, and a highly successful partnership was established in that country. Canada was the next objective; and the opposition were by now looking up. They decided that here was a battlefield on which Anton's group could be defeated. Admittedly it was a costly adventure in the early stages, but with great courage we won through and now enjoy a profitable business, having gained a substantial share of the Canadian market.

The next move was directed to Britain, and in 1958 our group acquired all the voting shares of Carreras Limited, which was the third in size among the English cigarette manufacturers. This company opened up new vistas for our group, as Carreras had factories in Fiji, Malta, Cyprus, and Jamaica. The company also acquired a large stake in Carrolls, a company in Ireland, in 1960. In 1965 Carreras acquired over 50% of the famous Alfred Dunhill Limited of London, and this association under the able chairmanship of my good friend, Mary Dunhill, has proved an excellent investment; and the Dunhill cigarette has now become a recognized world-wide quality brand.

Rhodesia was another country in which the powerful BAT decided to do their best to make our progress difficult. It was hard going to start with and a major price war took place. Before long we had lost a great deal of money and we were in fact losing on every cigarette we sold! But in the end we won through and now have about 50% of the total market.* From Rhodesia we moved to Zambia where we have been most successful. And in 1965 we joined forces with the Martin Brinkman group in Germany, now a leading company in the Rothmans Group. Besides all these operations we established companies in Holland and Switzerland and also purchased a small tobacco company called Larus in Richmond, Virginia. Rupert eventually formed a number of his companies into a big group called Rothmans International, which has proved a success.

With a view to diversifying our interests, Anton Rupert turned his attention to beer, and in 1967 an opportunity occurred in Canada to purchase 11% of the large company, Canadian Breweries. Eddie Taylor, the powerful Canadian financier and industrialist, agreed to dispose of his holding. In the past this shareholding had given him effective control. It was however clear that the same amount of shares in other hands might well make us vulnerable to a takeover bid. A year later this is exactly what happened. The large and successful American Tobacco Group, Phillip Morris, made a bid for 50% of the equity. We were faced with a very difficult situation, and it became a question of whether we should sell our shares and make a reasonable profit, or fight them for control. We chose the latter alternative as we still believed CBL provided us with just the right medium for diversification. We came to the conclusion that the best and cheapest way to go about it was to buy the additional shares we

---

* Owing to the Rhodesian situation, BAT and ourselves have had to agree to give up our usual cigarette packs and go it on the cheap.

needed to gain just over 50% on the open market. Our plans were carried out in the greatest secrecy and in spite of the hectic market activity no one knew for certain the real identity of the buyer. In June 1968 we won the battle, but there was much to be done, particularly in the United States where CBL possessed a wholly-owned subsidiary called Carling. This company was not making profits commensurate with the capital involved, although it was a well known and old-established brewery.

The expansion of our group has been really remarkable. Anton Rupert started the business with $28, and twenty years later the total assets were valued at more than $600 millions.

One can well ask how this success was achieved. In the first place it was due to Rupert's remarkable qualities. He possessed the qualities of a leader : courage and determination; also he was a good chooser and trainer of men. He had a flair for marketing and advertising and built a strong but small team around him, among whom were D. M. Hoogenhout, his financial controller, an able and very human person; and Dirk Hertzog, a nephew of the former South African Prime Minister. His two brothers are experts in the production and advertising fields. (I am called the international director, and I sit on a number of our boards around the world.) But probably the most important factor that helped his success was a new philosophy which he called industrial partnership.

This philosophy of industrial partnership deserves some further explanation. I will quote from Dr Rupert himself. This is how he summarizes it :

> We believe that we are the world's first truly 'multi-national' Group—a globe-encircling partnership of industrial companies in which at least 50% of the shares in each separate member company are held locally by nationals of the host country, and the chairmen and majority of board members in every country are citizens of that country. We believe that we have found a new formula of international understanding and co-operation through this system of complete and equal industrial partnership. Of the 1500 leading companies in the world we believe that ours is the only Group where chairmen and managing directors meet regularly around the conference table as 'complete equals'. We believe that we have given the world a new

concept of co-existence through shared mutual gain, and a new concept of world-orientation in business enterprise and business communication. We believe in true industrial partnership because we have seen it work.

By my standards Anton Rupert is a great man, a great South African. He is intensely human and the very opposite to what many people think leaders in the Republic are apt to be. He has a very kindly approach to the difficult problems that exist in his country and besides his strictly business interests his activities are legion. Being a lover of the arts he has acquired unique collections of pictures, sculptures and tapestries. He also finds time to play an active part in the World Wildlife Foundation. The ex-President, Prince Bernhard of the Netherlands, will be the first to acknowledge this. As a demonstration of his desire to help the less developed peoples, he accepted the appointment of honorary industrial adviser to Chief Jonathan of Lesotho, where he has done much to help this impoverished small country. Amongst other things he has been instrumental in organizing visits to Lesotho by various people from South Africa, including medical specialists, nurses, agricultural and other experts—the Medical Shuttle Service having now celebrated its tenth anniversary and more than 20,000 man-hours of free medical work.

On arrival in London Anton Rupert told me that a problem had arisen in Carreras, the British group which we controlled. A serious difference of opinion had developed on certain issues between the board and the chairman and managing director. This was particularly unfortunate as he was a personal friend of mine, and he had achieved considerable success in running the company. The upshot was that we agreed to part company, so the serious problem of finding a new chairman arose.

As an interim measure Anton Rupert, who served on the Carreras board, agreed to take over the chair, but because of his world-wide commitments it was patently impossible for him to devote enough time to this. He therefore asked me to join the board as his deputy. As there appeared to be no other immediate answer, I agreed. This meant I was stuck in London for the time being. After a few weeks I started to make noises about returning to South Africa, after which pressure was put on to get me to become chairman for a considerable length of time. Having experienced this sort of thing before under TI and because of my age, I declined the invitation. One evening Anton and I were dining alone in his flat at Grosvenor House, when he appealed to me to help him out as he could think of no other answer. He is a persuasive man and as I owed him so much, I agreed—though reluctantly—to become chairman for a maximum of eighteen months. This meant being away from my home, friends and servants in the Republic, but in the end I saw it had to be.

I found myself in the familiar role of healing wounds and taking on a job that was new to me. It was only natural that the late chairman's departure had rocked the ship to some extent and this had resulted in pro and anti ex-chairman factions. A firm grip had to be taken and morale restored as soon as possible. I made a point of meeting as many of the executives and staff as I could and travelled round the country in order to get to know those who worked 'in the field'. I remain extremely grateful for the way I was received and the many kindnesses I experienced. Before long I began really to enjoy myself and the challenge this assignment presented.

I still did quite a lot of travelling, but at this stage it was confined mainly to Europe and North America. I had the opportunity to renew old friendships in the UK and also managed to fit in a certain amount of shooting. In the cigarette business one gets involved in numerous sponsorships such as tennis, golf and cricket, as well as in the spheres of music and art. So one's life was a pretty full one. Nevertheless I enjoyed the experience, and the profits for my first full year as chairman were very satisfactory; they increased by nearly 50%. I'm not suggesting that this was owing to my arrival, as part of the success was due to plans that had been prepared beforehand. I can at least say that I helped to keep the ship on an even keel during what could have been a very difficult period.

Despite my return to Britain and my many responsibilities in Europe, I never ceased to try and do my best for the country which had 'adopted' me after the war—and whose soldiers had fought and died so bravely for our ideals. It was in 1958 that I and some friends of mine, including that fine citizen, Eric Gallo, started off the South Africa Foundation. Its object was to try and keep the Republic's image a good one overseas and bring about some harmony between the races in the country itself. We attacked the double standards which were employed against us, explained the history and achievements of the white man in South Africa. We formed a man-to-man movement which consisted of committees of the various countries whose citizens lived in the country, and we invited well-known statesmen, industrialists, financiers, etc. to visit us as our guests, at our expense. We never tried to muzzle them, let them go where they liked and talk to whom they wished. They could also say what they liked when they left the country. This proved remarkably successful, and the list of our guests is really quite formidable.

We naturally had to raise a lot of money and the organization is now financially very secure. I remember visiting the late Lord Nelson in London with a view to obtaining a reasonable sum of money. But he was not keen and he said he was sure we would become political and that would break the Foundation up. But I assured him that whilst I was president I would never let this happen, and that we would ensure that we did not become a whitewashing organization that set out to back up entirely government policy. However, we kept in close touch with the Government and let them know the views we found overseas, which I think proved helpful to them.

We naturally stressed that the present policies stemmed from the time of British control of the Union, and that Britain had given freedom and independence to the protectorates which was precisely what South Africa had now given to the Transkei and proposed to extend the policy to areas inhabited by other racial groups. Yet Britain had not recognized the Transkei.

Travelling around the world as I did, I took the opportunity of discussing the problem with many of the world's leaders: Eisenhower, Richard Nixon, Sir Alec Douglas-Home, Selwyn Lloyd, George Brown, Denis Healey, Edward Heath, Dr Luns of the Netherlands, Lester Pearson, Pierre Trudeau, Dean Rusk, Senator Mike Mansfield, McGeorge Bundy, Henry Kissinger and many others. Some at least agreed to come to South Africa as uncommitted guests of our Foundation and see conditions as they really are; all were interested to hear what Ike called 'the convictions of a thoughtful, patriotic and western-oriented man who happens to live in South Africa'. The fact that I never surrendered my British passport undoubtedly gave me a certain independence and impartiality. Ill health stopped Eisenhower from making his intended trip to South Africa; in the meantime he declared: 'Except for what you have told me about South Africa I am not sufficiently acquainted with the area to make any judgement and I have sense enough not to attempt it. I have been impressed by South Africa's gallant participation in two world wars and I must say that if ever trouble arose again in which my country were involved I would like to have South African units on my side.' He abhorred the 'holier than thou' attitude which so many liberals affected—particularly those 'ambitious politicians' concerned only 'to win over the Negro vote in this country. Yet there is plenty of evidence that the measures and policies we have tried to apply in this country in equalizing opportunity for the Negro have been notable for their failures more than for their successes.' In 1966 he wrote to me:

Scarcely a week passes that I am not writing to some American friend of mine urging more study of the South African situation before he makes some pronouncement about the problems and situation of that country as they now exist. Time and again I point out to such a person that he is not omnipotent; that until he has made a thorough study of South Africa on the ground, he is in no position to even express an opinion, much less a recommendation.

It is easy to see how Eisenhower, by his integrity and compassion, elicited such loyalty.

Monty's attitude towards South Africa was altogether bolder and more controversial—as befitted the man he was. Where others sympathized privately and dared say nothing publicly (or did not sympathize publicly but could offer privately no constructive suggestions as to what they would do in the same situation) Montgomery took ship and came to see for himself a second time in 1962. He stayed with my colleague Slip Menell and toured the entire country, making many friends. I arranged most of the three-week itinerary; and marvelled at the way Montgomery detailed all his needs and questions to me by letter, in his own hand, without ever employing a secretary.

Will it be hot in Cape Town, Umtala and Durban? [he enquired three months before departure, having bought his ticket] I would propose to bring:
One decent suit
Dinner jacket
Flannel trousers, and cotton jacket
and sports coat.
Will this be OK?
And do I not need some form of overcoat; or will a light raincoat do?

Montgomery had been a distinguished staff officer in the First World War; allied with his almost schoolboyish fetish about lists of all sorts this produced a meticulous approach to planning that was not always easy to satisfy—as I well knew!

He much enjoyed his trip; but when he tried to write about it at home in England—he was contractually tied to the *Sunday Times*—he found great difficulty in getting his views published. The editor, he wrote to me,

is frightened of getting the *Sunday Times* involved in the South Africa problem in view of the present climate of opinion against that country in the UK and in UNO. It is typical of the Press; when one writes the truth, as I have, they won't publish it; when one tells lies, they publish them. In fact, they won't try and educate public opinion to see the facts.

Monty tried to get the *Daily Telegraph* to run his articles, as well as a BBC discussion with himself and Van Schoor; but two weeks later he wrote despondently: 'The articles have been refused by the *Telegraph* . . . My agent is pursuing other papers, but I rather think I shall call him off.' To which he added, in red ink: 'Note: I *have* called him off.' The BBC declined to broadcast the discussion Montgomery wanted; but by mid-March 1962 he reported:

The *Sunday Times* relented, and an article on the Transkei, and my talks with tribal chiefs and Luthuli is coming out to-morrow . . . I am now going to write a book about China,

South Africa and Central America, and the two articles will appear in full in that. The book will be called *Three Continents* and will have a chapter at the end on defence.

Despite the attacks made on him in political circles and in the Press, Montgomery never faltered in his admiration for South Africa, and his conviction that it constituted the cornerstone in Western defence against communism. Thereafter he gave up his annual trips to Switzerland, and instead spent the worst weeks of the unspeakable English winter journeying to South Africa, where I always met, dined, and often sailed part of the passage with him. He admitted that some of the methods of the South African Government 'do seem a bit clumsy at times', but felt sure that over the years the 'world should begin to see that the broad philosophy of the Nationalist Government is right'.

The following year he began to interest himself in South African defence, beginning with its cadet schools which he visited.

The cadet material is good [he wrote to me]. But they have only the remotest idea of what is going on in the world; and they don't study history sufficiently; too much attention to the cash value of education (getting a degree) and too little on learning how to go on teaching themselves as they grow up.

By this time the Field-Marshal was fast approaching his eighties; yet he was still anxious to go up in a helicopter to study the Natal beaches 'with a view to its suitability or otherwise for assault landings by an enemy'. He was forced into a situation where the *Sunday Times* would only publish articles on defence aspects of South Africa, which disappointed him; but I gradually managed to get his complete articles published in South Africa itself; and he continued to make his annual trip to Cape Town. At the end of 1966 he admonished me: 'I have a feeling that you do too much—travelling round the world at your age!' I was then sixty-six; coming from a man entering his eightieth year it was a bit much! Yet the following May he went on the *Sunday Times* pilgrimage to Alamein and saw Nasser; and planned a further trip to South Africa early in 1968.

It was at this juncture, on his eightieth birthday, that he

suffered perhaps the most unexpected and most unexpectedly shattering blow. His old VCIGS, General Sir Frank Simpson, had organized an eightieth birthday party in the banqueting hall of the Chelsea Royal Hospital, where Simpson was then the Governor. Monty came and was in his best form, mellow and obviously pleased to meet his old friends. We enjoyed a wonderful dinner and talked late into the night. Monty had arranged to stay the night at the Hospital, but early next morning he received a phone call from his home in Hampshire giving him most distressing news. His house had been burgled during the night and most of his silver had been stolen, including many of the beautiful presentations that had been given him when he had received the freedom of a number of cities. His Field-Marshal's baton was also stolen. They were of course irreplaceable and he never got them back. It is too tragic to think that these magnificent trophies were probably all melted down merely for the value of the metal. Montgomery was terribly upset and cancelled his intended voyage to South Africa that winter; but there was nothing he could do about the loss.

In time, however, Montgomery recovered. The following year saw the publication of his monumental *History of Warfare* at the age of eighty-one, and he even proposed to sail to Australia and New Zealand. I cautioned him, and advised a proper medical examination before embarking on anything so ambitious.

I took your advice [he wrote in the summer of 1968], and had a very thorough overhaul by a team of specialists at the Cambridge Hospital, Aldershot. They could find nothing wrong with me. But in view of my past medical history they said that things could easily go wrong, under strain. Their considered opinion was that I must not make the visit, and this opinion admitted of no qualification whatsoever.

Later that year, just after his eighty-first birthday, my fears were borne out—and Montgomery collapsed in the House of Lords, while carrying the Sword of State. 'I recovered quickly when taken to an open window. A glass of champagne helped!'

Yet still he refused to give up; and in January 1969 he was writing to me with plans to sail and spend Christmas and New Year 1970 with the Governor-General of New Zealand, Arthur

Porritt, and thenceforth 'resume my visits to Cape Town' every January!

Age however was closing in on him; and wisely he withdrew more and more into the privacy and serenity of his beautiful converted mill in Hampshire.

That year—1969—Eisenhower himself succumbed to old age and the strains which a long and noble life had placed upon him. I was invited to the funeral by the Eisenhower family as a special guest—but my own doctor now forbade me fly the long journey, and regretfully I missed the opportunity of paying my last homage to an old and constant friend. I had however contributed to *The Times'* obituary that was being rewritten only a few months before : a homage of a different but perhaps more lasting kind. 'Ike was so proud of your friendship,' Mamie wrote afterwards; and in a PS had added : 'He always wanted to visit South Africa and Australia.' To know my friendship had been valued by such a distinguished figure in the world was indeed a humbling realization.

It was a thousand pities that Montgomery and Eisenhower were never reconciled—though I did my best to achieve it. Monty's ability to command his health was remarkable considering the severity of his First World War wounds; like Churchill he survived by an effort of the same indomitable will that had characterized his life. However, in the end he too succumbed, dying comfortably in his sleep some seven years after Eisenhower. Once again I was invited as a family guest to the funeral—indeed as pall-bearer from the barracks in Windsor to St George's Chapel, where the coffin was to lie in state before final burial at Binstead, near Monty's home.

My legs were giving me a lot of trouble and I was shortly due to have an operation on my right leg. I was also rather weak from radio-therapy treatment for a tumour in my head. When summoned by the War Department to report for this duty, I rang up my doctor in London—Cecil Eppel—asking his advice. He thought my leg rather insecure, but I told him that he must see me through. This he did and arrived at where I was staying in London just before I left for Windsor and gave me a king-size injection and pills to take during the day.

When we set off from the barracks in Windsor for the long march to St George's Chapel, I flung my stick away and got going. After a while I noticed that a large guardsman was marching on my left, but on looking round I noticed that the other pall-bearers had no such attention. So at a convenient moment I turned to this chap and asked him what he was doing. He looked straight in front of him and did not reply. But on my return to the barracks I asked a friend of mine what this soldier had been there for. The reply I received was, 'Oh, in case you flaked out!' In point of fact I managed the assignment without trouble and was glad that I could pay this, my last tribute to my old Chief.

What a strange character he had been, I reflected that evening. Some of his behaviour towards me had defied belief—and could only be understood in the context of his peculiar, somehow always insecure genius. From the time I was a junior subaltern in the mess at York in 1922 he had shown an interest in my future; had encouraged me to take my profession seriously, helped me to get into Staff College and, ultimately, had given me the chance of a lifetime in the desert in August 1942. During those historic years he had—as I have written in *Generals at War* —constantly shown an almost fatherly concern for my health and even my happiness. In his *Memoirs* he repeatedly ascribed to me a major share in his great military success; and in July 1958 he insisted that I be present at the farewell banquet to be given him by the Army Council on his retirement that autumn: 'I told the War Office that anything I may have been able to achieve during the late war could not have been done if you had not been at my side. One cannot do these things alone.'

Yet this same man had sometimes been so wounding. He asked me not to take on the rank of my predecessor, Lieutenant-General Morgan, when I became Chief of Staff, 21st Army Group, early in 1944; and despite a knighthood in the field I remained a Major-General until the German surrender. Imagine, then, my consternation when, two months after the war was over, I read in the *London Gazette* that I had been reduced to the substantive rank of Colonel! Nothing I said to Montgomery would persuade him to act on my behalf—and it was only when Eisenhower heard about the case and made angry protestations to Alan Brooke, then CIGS, that I was given the substantive rank of Major-General.

Montgomery's attitude towards my promotion and awards was

certainly bound up in his complex psychology. He would not permit me to be present at the signing of the German surrender in his tent on Lüneburg Heath; nor did he invite me to the victory parade in Whitehall thereafter; nor was I given or permitted to receive any military awards after the Normandy campaign. Yet having decided I must become VCIGS when he took over Brooke's job after the war, he cut short my convalescence and forced me to take the post of DMI at the War Office immediately in the summer of 1945. When in 1946 he was advised that my appointment as VCIGS might smack too much of the 'old team', he changed his mind. This was entirely within his rights; but the manner in which he informed me was, to say the least, bizarre. I was in my office in Whitehall when the door was thrust open and Montgomery popped his head inside. Seeing that I was engaged—I was talking to General Sir Bernard Freyberg, VC—he asked me to step outside. Without preliminaries he said, 'Oh, Freddie, I've decided not to have you as my Vice.' I asked him why not, and he replied, 'Because it wouldn't do me any good.' With no more ado he then left!

Bernard Freyberg, who had heard the brief conversation and knew of my coming appointment as VCIGS, said, 'Did I hear correctly?' Still stunned, I replied, 'I think so.' 'The little bugger!' Freyberg commented.

That evening I wrote to Monty, asking for a more forthcoming explanation of this sudden change of mind. The reason he had given me was really so insulting that I couldn't help but feel hurt, for it suggested that, in the view of other War Office officials, I would not be a competent Vice, or perhaps was untrustworthy. It certainly didn't say much for Monty's position and prestige in Whitehall that he should cut his coat to suit his cloth.

Three days later Montgomery replied. He answered me that 'our association would be quoted for years to come as an example of complete trust and confidence. Of that there is no doubt.' The problem, he explained, was this:

> If I take you on as Vice, the Army will say that I am collecting in the old gang again and that no one will have any future unless he is one of my chaps. That would never do. I have already put in Kirkie and Lyme, and all my old Corps Comds

are now in the Home Commands. Future appointments will be watched and criticised.

If it were war, I would not care what anyone said.

But it is Peace, and there is a herculean job ahead.

I can have only one yardstick: the best interests of the Army.

If I considered only my own interests I would put you straight in as Vice. But I have decided that I must not do so. Do not make it any harder for me by 'bellyaching'.

No one has ever had, or ever will have, a more loyal and devoted Chief of Staff than you were. If we go to war again in my time, I would put you straight in as Chief of Staff.

I hope above is clear.

It was, and I said nothing further; but the feeling that envious tongues had spoken against me (I was still only forty-five) and that Montgomery had listened to them hurt me deeply. We remained friends, as I hope this manuscript testifies; but even in subsequent years he could resort to strange behaviour at times. When the time came for his eightieth birthday party he excluded me from the list of invitations; and only when Sir Miles Dempsey found out and protested did I receive an invitation. So disgusted was Dempsey that he then refused to attend himself! Moreover, the following year when the *Sunday Times* paid for Montgomery to visit the Alamein battlefields, he would not permit the editor, Denis Hamilton, to invite me. 'It is a very small party, and a very "closed shop",' he wrote to me when I asked if what I'd heard was true—I, his Chief of Staff during the very battle!

I was bitterly hurt by this obviously quite conscious slight. When Eisenhower heard about it, he wrote that he shared my sadness 'over the abominable treatment you have received from a man who has every reason to feel deeply obligated to you for long years of service. Indeed I have often wondered how you found it possible to be so tolerant toward the whole affair.'

As I accompanied Monty's dead body the long way to St George's Chapel, I too wondered.

I suppose the answer was: to anyone with eyes to see and ears to listen, to anyone who had been involved with the British Army between 1919 and 1945 he was, indisputably, the greatest military field commander our nation managed to produce. Only Slim came anywhere near him in this respect. Montgomery's was a strange genius—but genius it was. Unlike Alexander, whose reputation was made largely by the media, Monty was a self-made man who seized his chance when Britain's fortunes seemed at their lowest ebb. He commanded men's loyalty because he was so utterly, ruthlessly professional; and if he has been accused of being unimaginative, this may be because he made imagination almost redundant by his very professionalism. And yet he was so strangely insecure in his fame, occasionally so threatened, almost as a child! Perhaps all really great men have their warts; these were some of Monty's which I acknowledged and bore because his greatness as a soldier so outweighed them. He never possessed Eisenhower's breadth of vision, transparent humility or nobility; but at the deadly business of war, the task of making a largely amateur army first equal with, then superior to, a highly disciplined, indoctrinated enemy he had no rival. I was proud that he had asked that I should be one of his pall-bearers—that at least this one 'occasion' be not denied me.

Age however had crept up on me as well; and I began gradually to cut down my business responsibilities.

We were fortunate in persuading Sir Derek Pritchard (now Lord Pritchard) to join the Carreras group and become the next chairman. He was a man after my own heart. He had been the very successful chairman of Allied Breweries. He was also chairman of the British Export Council and recently was elected president of the Institute of Directors. As the newspapers commented at the time, we were pretty good at swopping chairmen, having had five in a very few years; but in spite of this Carreras has advanced from strength to strength.

It will be seen therefore that my joining Dr Anton Rupert's group rather late in life didn't result in an easier existence but on the contrary, a very active one. By leaving the army when I did, I had assured myself some twenty-five years of new life in the exacting world of business and commerce. Moreover, my friendships with Eisenhower, Montgomery, Bedell Smith and other colleagues from the time of the Second World War had enabled me to remain in touch with the profession in which I had trained and in which I had risen to heights never dreamed of in my youth. I had, indeed, had the 'best of both worlds'.

I'm now in the happy position of being as busy as I wish to be, but at the age of seventy-eight one sometimes finds the spirit is willing but the flesh is weak.

I can still travel to many lands, fish and shoot and play bridge with my friends. I have enjoyed my life and although the old saying that 'old soldiers never die' is somewhat inaccurate, nevertheless I hope I may still have some happy years ahead.

Index

Reynolds, Louis, 93
Reynolds, Richard, 93
Reynolds Metals, 88, 91, 93
Rhodes, Cecil John, 69, 70
Rice, Walter, 92
Richdale, Gordon, 45
Rickaby, Fred, 73
Robins, Colonel Sir Ellis, 24, 25
Robinson, Bill, 91
Rommel, Field Marshal, 4, 5, 9, 10
Rothmans International, 103
Rothmans of Pall Mall, 102
Rupert, Dr Anton, 66, 98, 99, 100,
    101–6

Sasolberg, 41
Scribner, Charles, 36
SHAEF (Supreme Headquarters
    Allied Expeditionary Force), 17,
    90
SHAPE (Supreme Headquarters
    Allied Powers in Europe), 79
shooting, 69–70
Simplex company, 58
Simpson, General Sir Frank 'Simbo',
    7, 16, 17, 111
Slim, Field Marshal, 115–16
Smith, General Bedell, 32, 38; en-
    gagement, 38–9
Smuts, Field Marshal Jan, 26, 32,
    40, 65
South Africa Foundation, 98, 106–8
Springs: factory at, see Ace Cycle
    and Engineering Company; foun-
    dry at, 58–60
Stedeford, Sir Ivan, 49, 56, 80, 97;
    first meetings, 50–1; in S. Africa,

53–5; injury in France, 58; and
    Raleigh Industries, 62–3, 96; and
    British Aluminium, 88; disagree-
    ment with author, 99–100
Stevens, 'Texas', 20
Stirling, Bill, 30
Stirling, David, 30, 41, 42, 43, 46
Suez crisis, 82–4
Sunday Times, 109, 110
Sunlit Years, The (Richdale), 45
Suzman, Helen, 72

Tedder, Air Marshal, 13, 46
Trudeau, Pierre, 94
Tube Investments (*see* also Stede-
    ford, Sir Ivan): and Ace Cycle
    Company, 49–56, 59–60; S.
    African Operations, 58, 76; and
    Hercules Cycle Company, 61;
    author's deputy chairman pro-
    posal, 80–2; and British Alumin-
    ium, 88–91; and Raleigh Indus-
    tries, 62–3, 96; and unions, 97

unions, negotiations with, 97
United Party, 72
Usher, Sir George, 68

Voelker, John, 68

Wavell, General, 3–4
Welensky, Sir Roy, 26
wholesalers, cycle, 52, 60
Wilson, George, 63, 96, 97
Windsor, Duke and Duchess of, 19

yacht, aluminium, 94–6